Adult Coloring Book
Featuring Cats, Romance, Angels, & Flowers

By Laura L. Smith

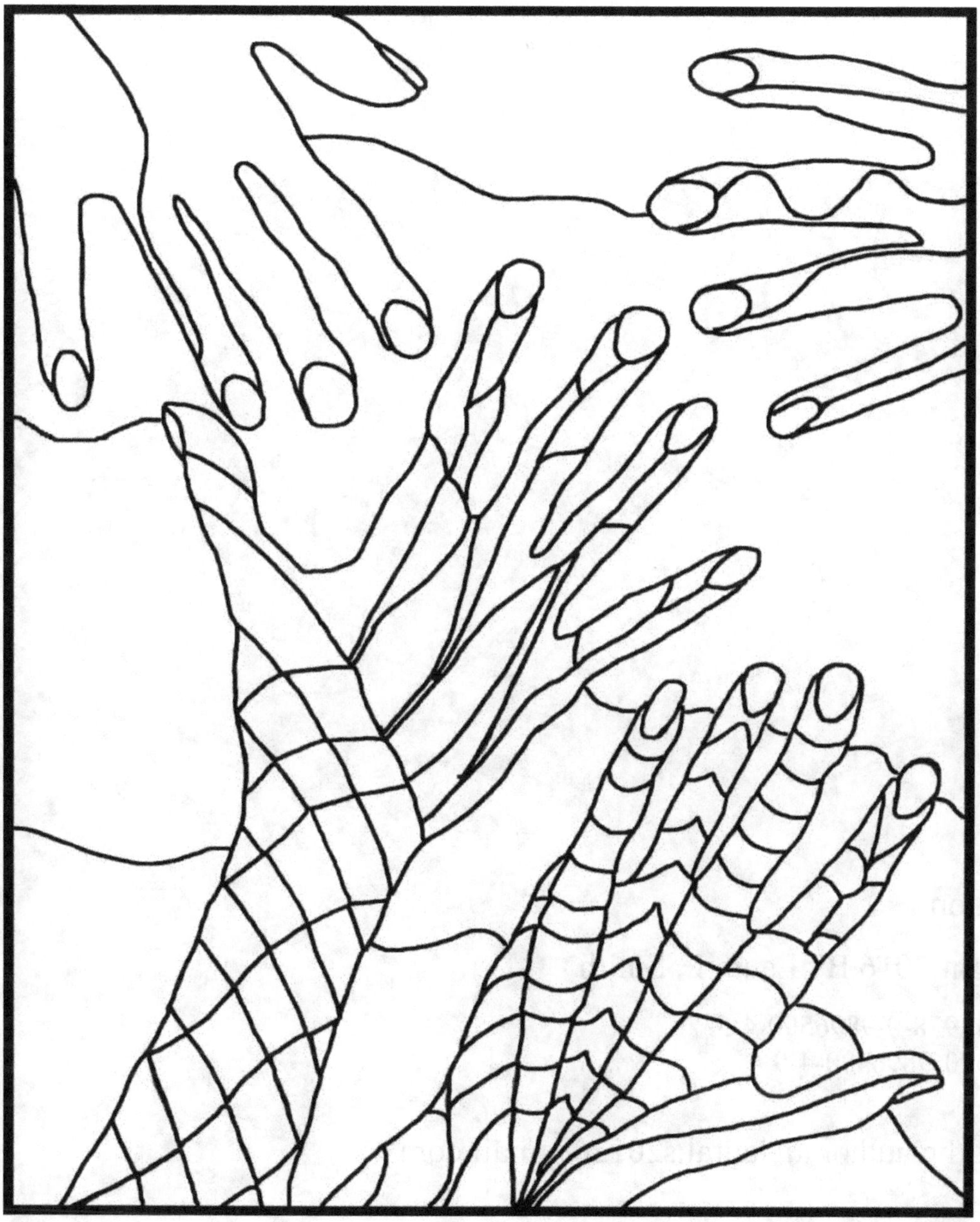

This coloring book features more than 50 drawings of cats, romantic scenes, angel's, and flowers. The diverse and abstract drawings give the colorist the opportunity to use their coloring imagination. Appropriate for framing.

1st Edition

Copyright 2016 By Laura L. Smith

ISBN-13: 978-0-9896500-4-5
ISBN-10: 0-9896500-4-9

Contact the author @ laural.s2012@gmail.com

All illustrations by Laura L. Smith

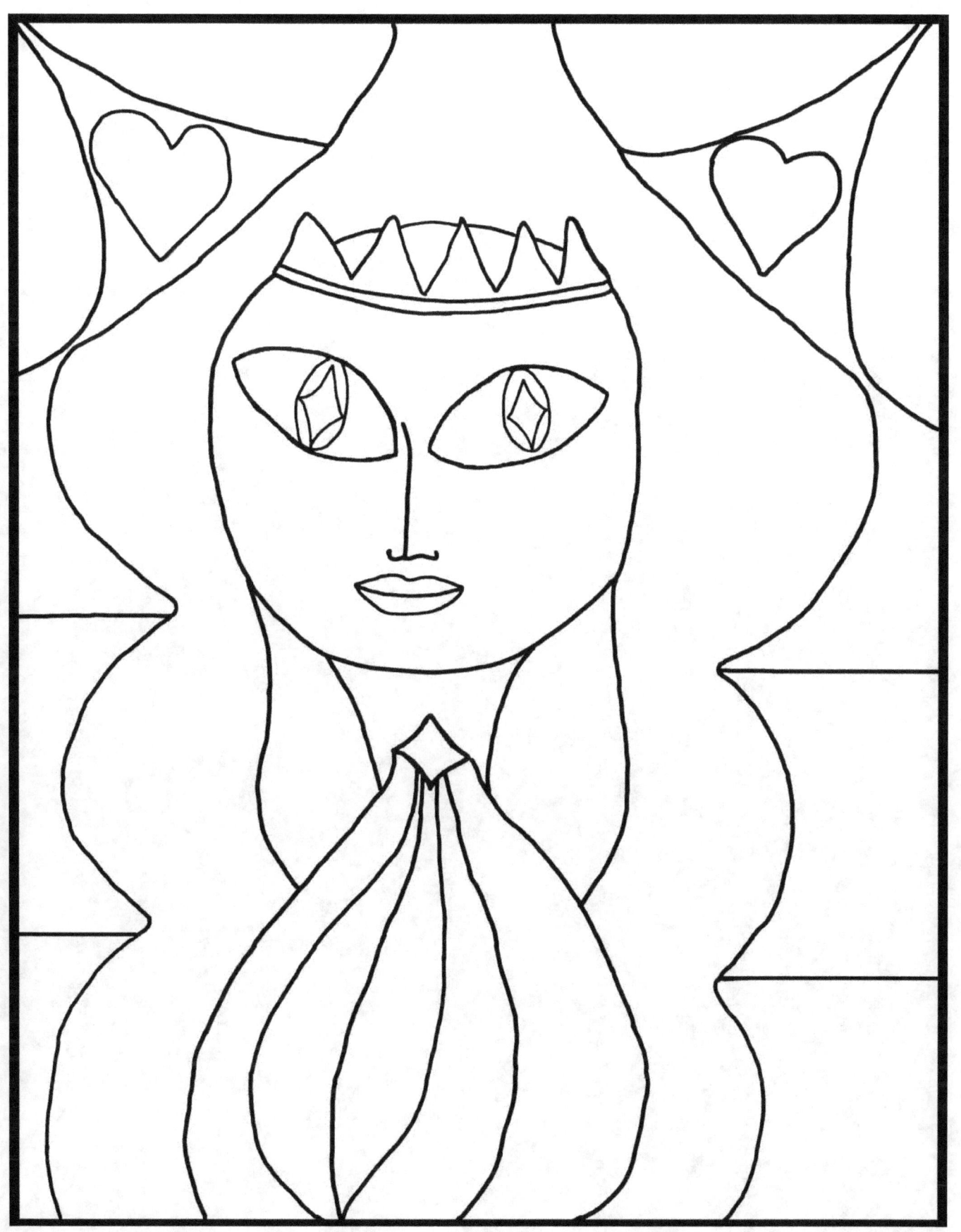

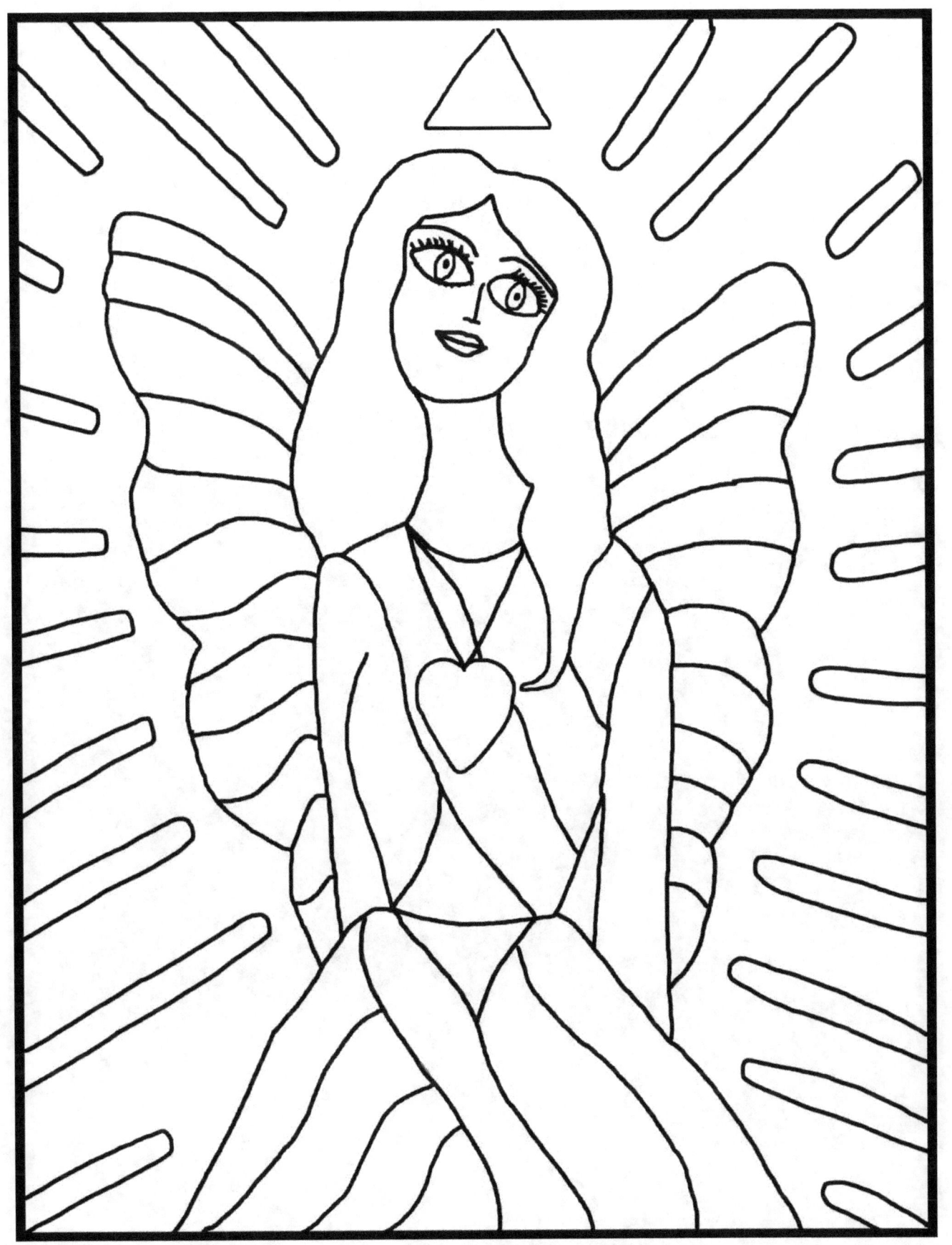

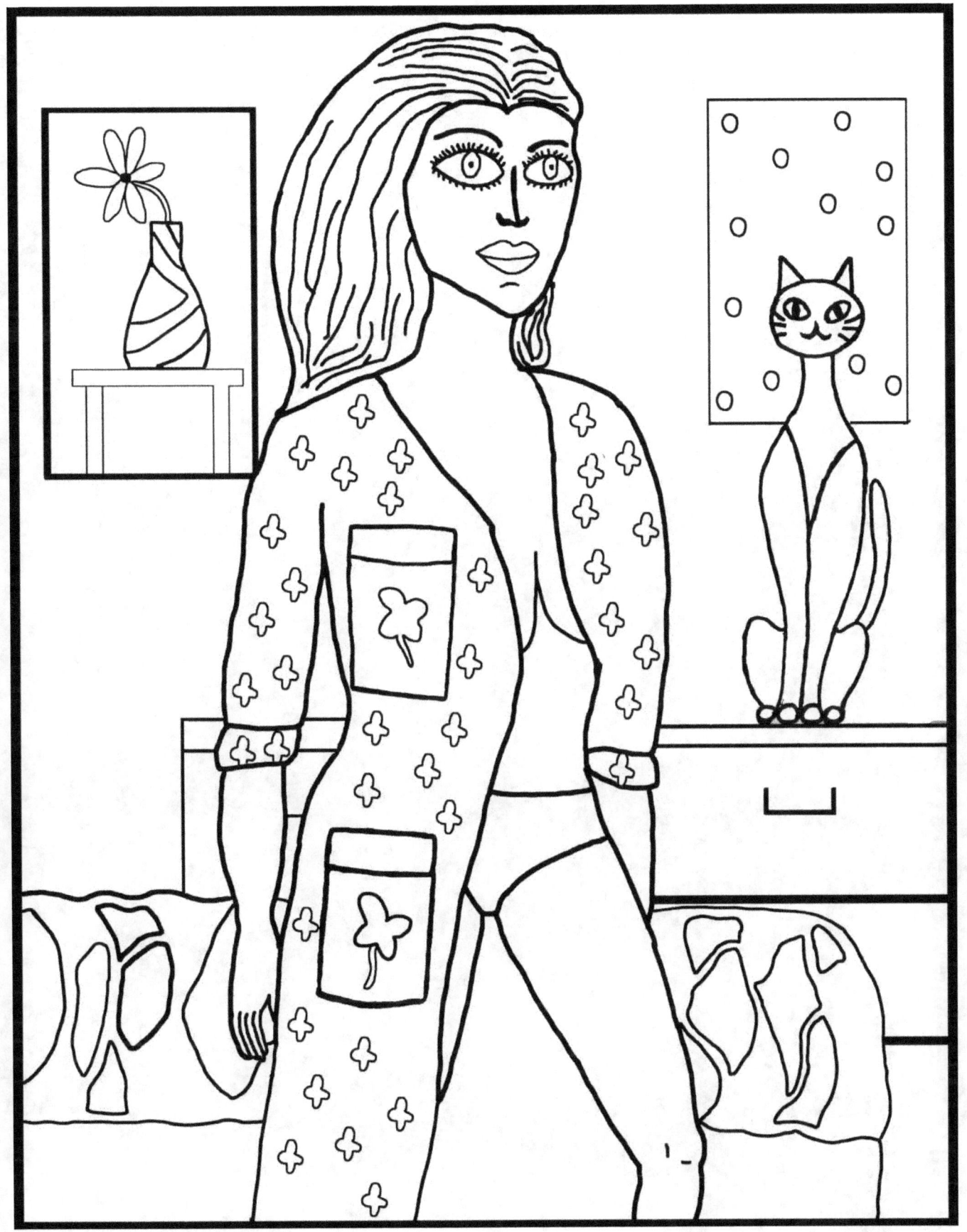

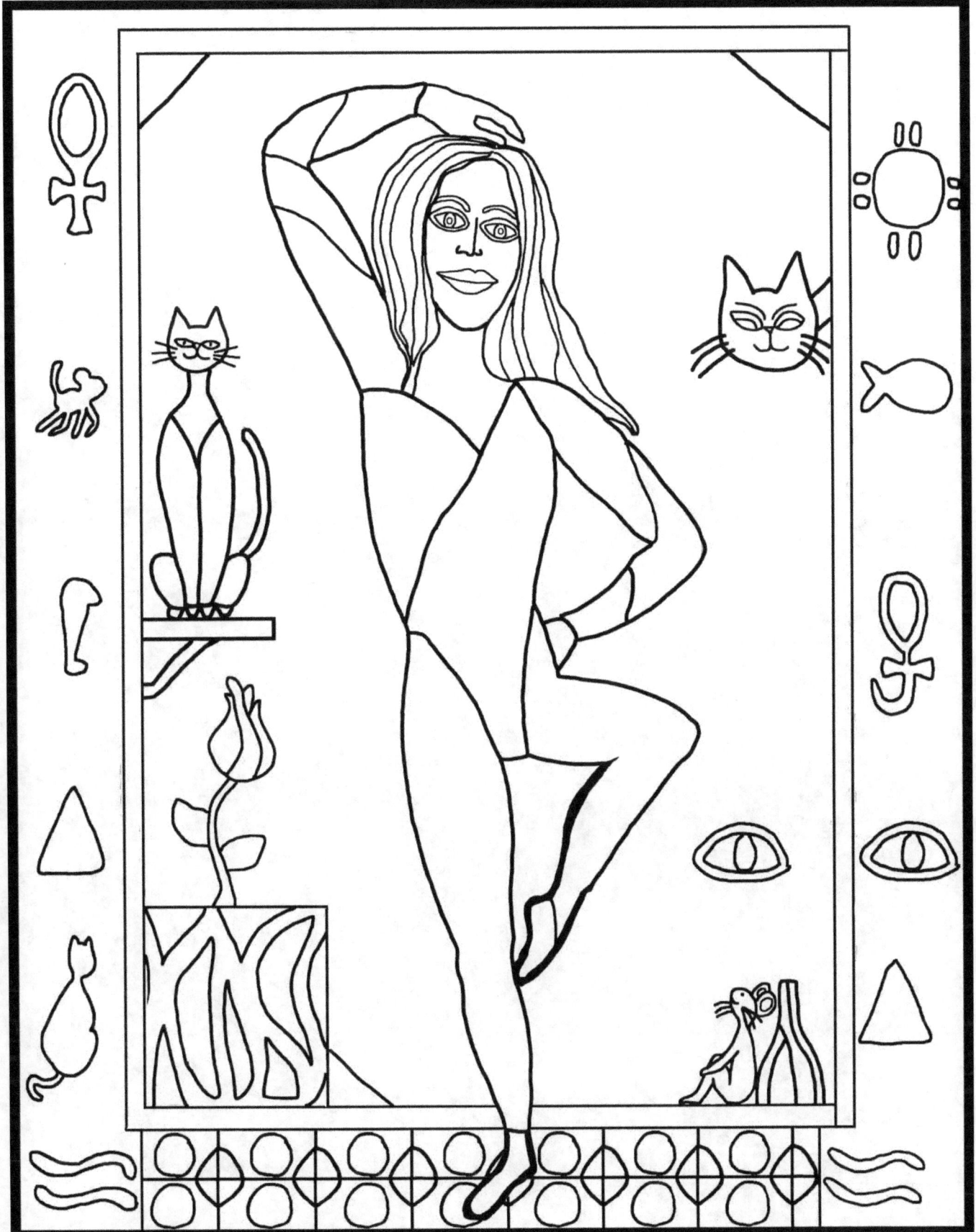

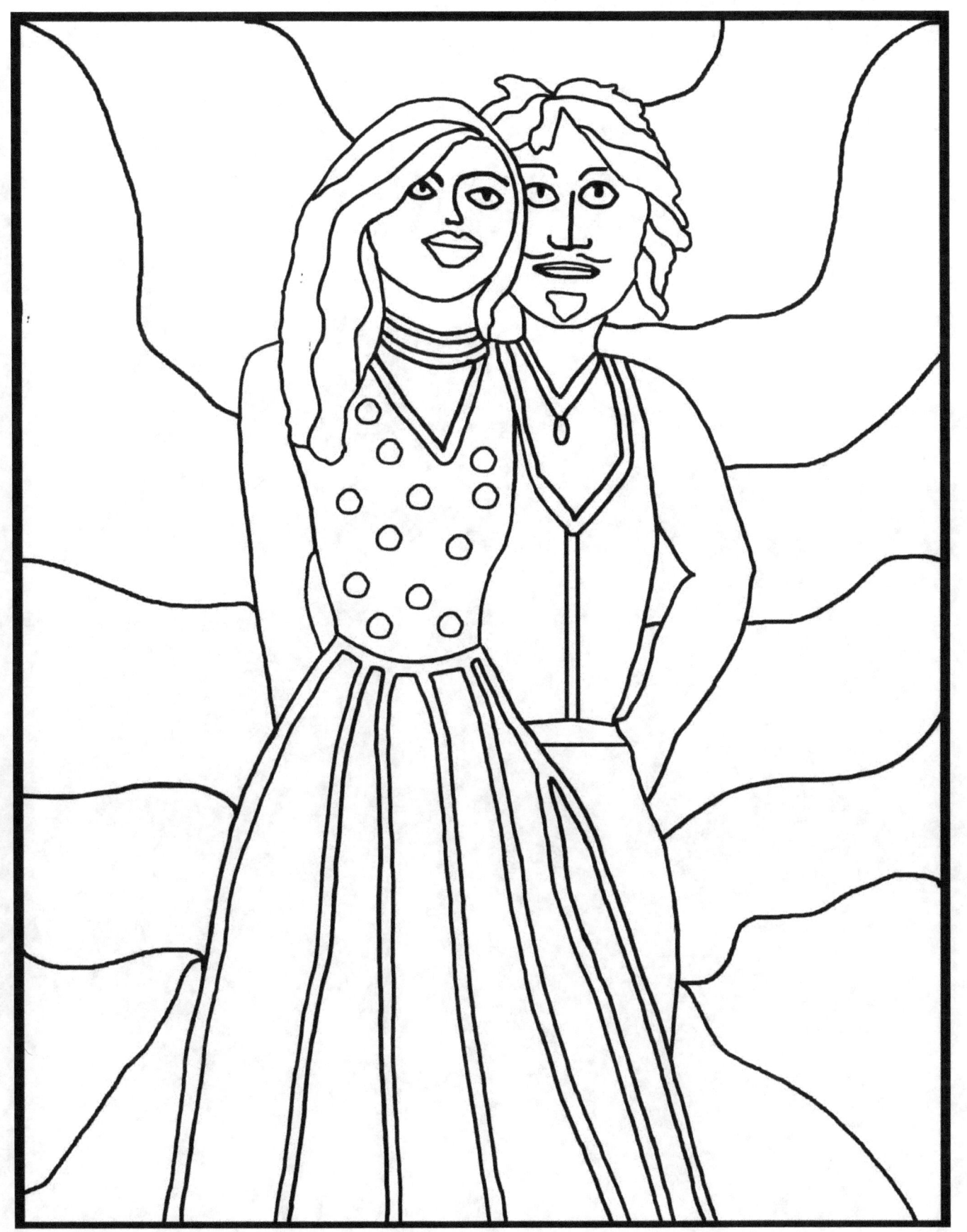

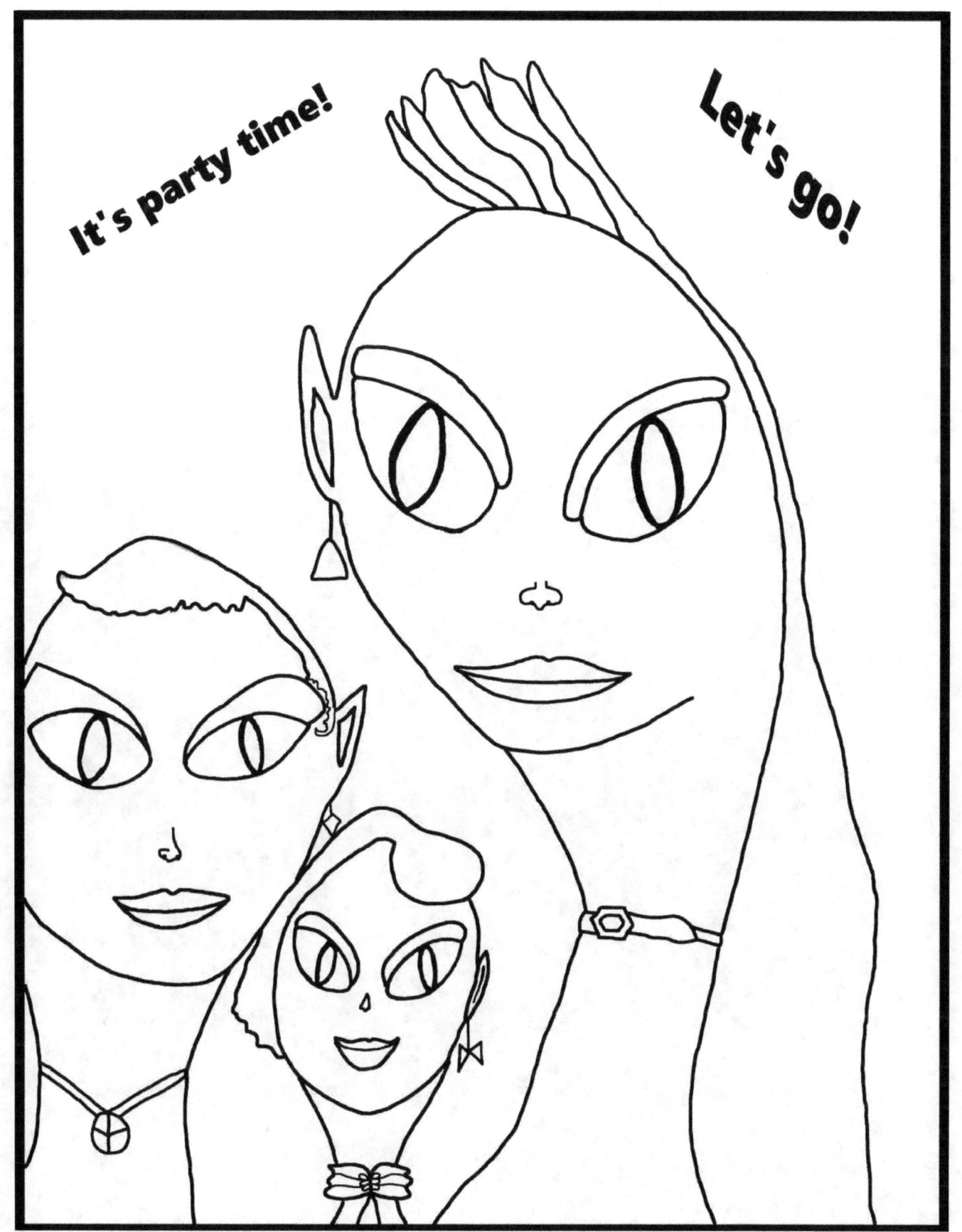

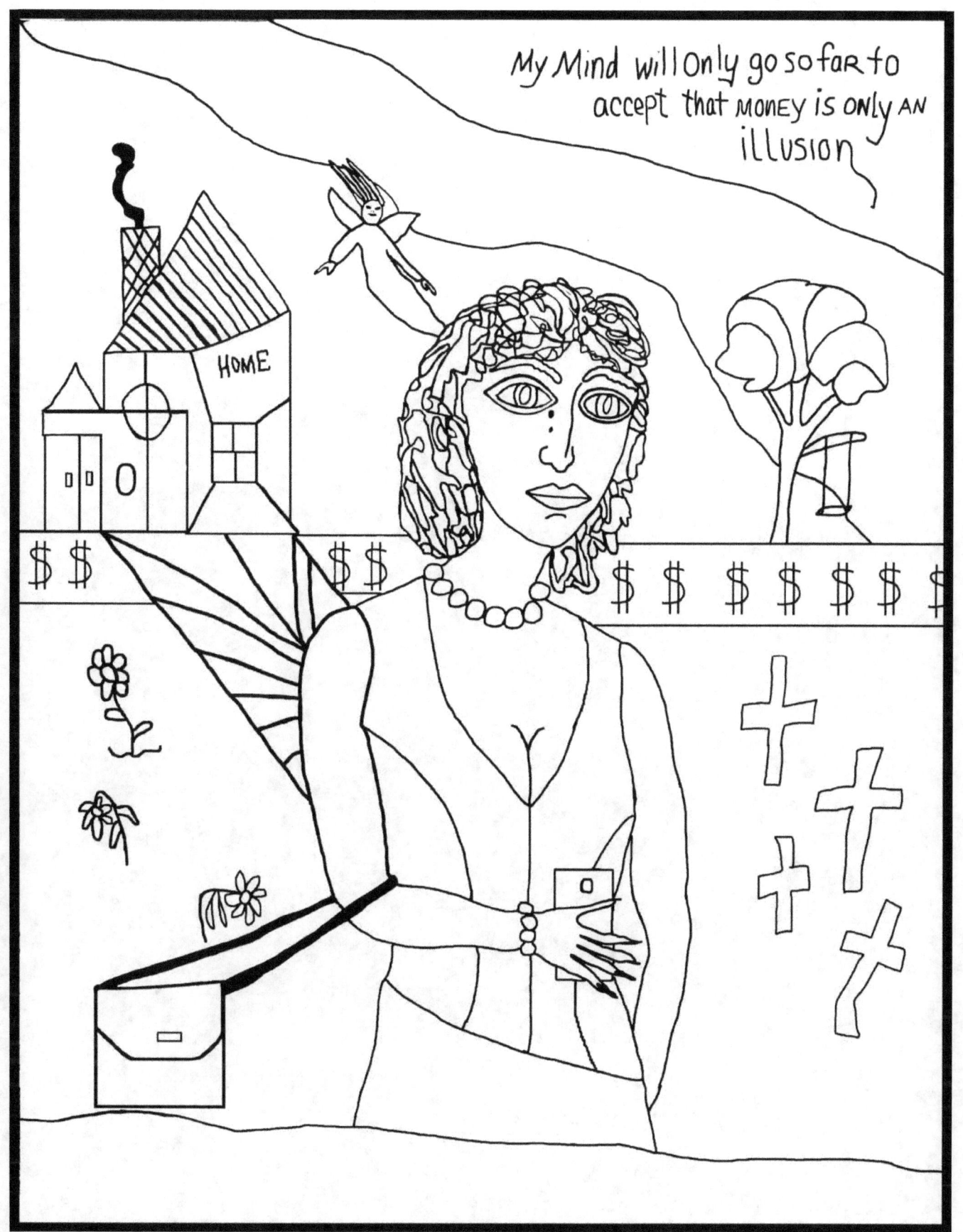

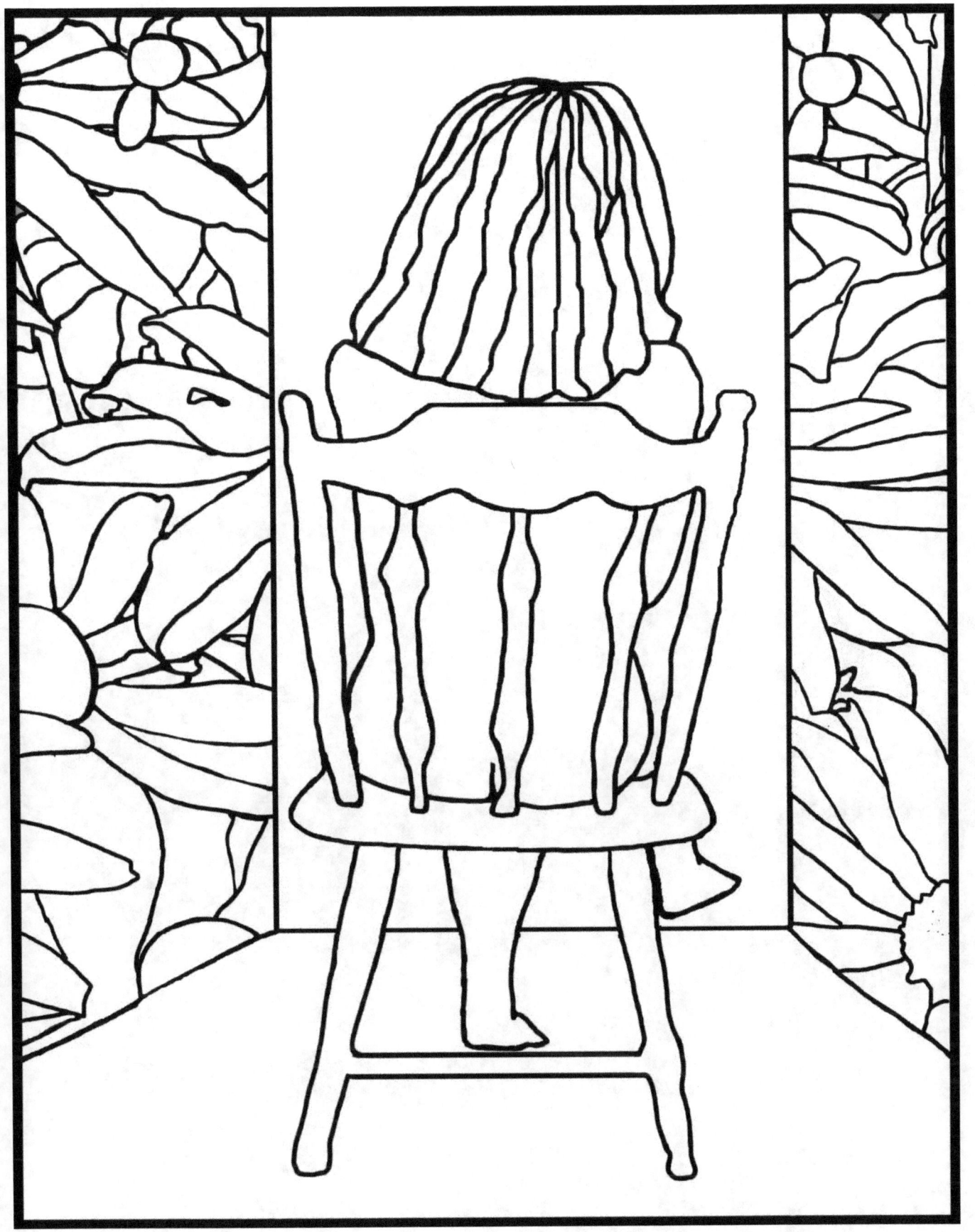

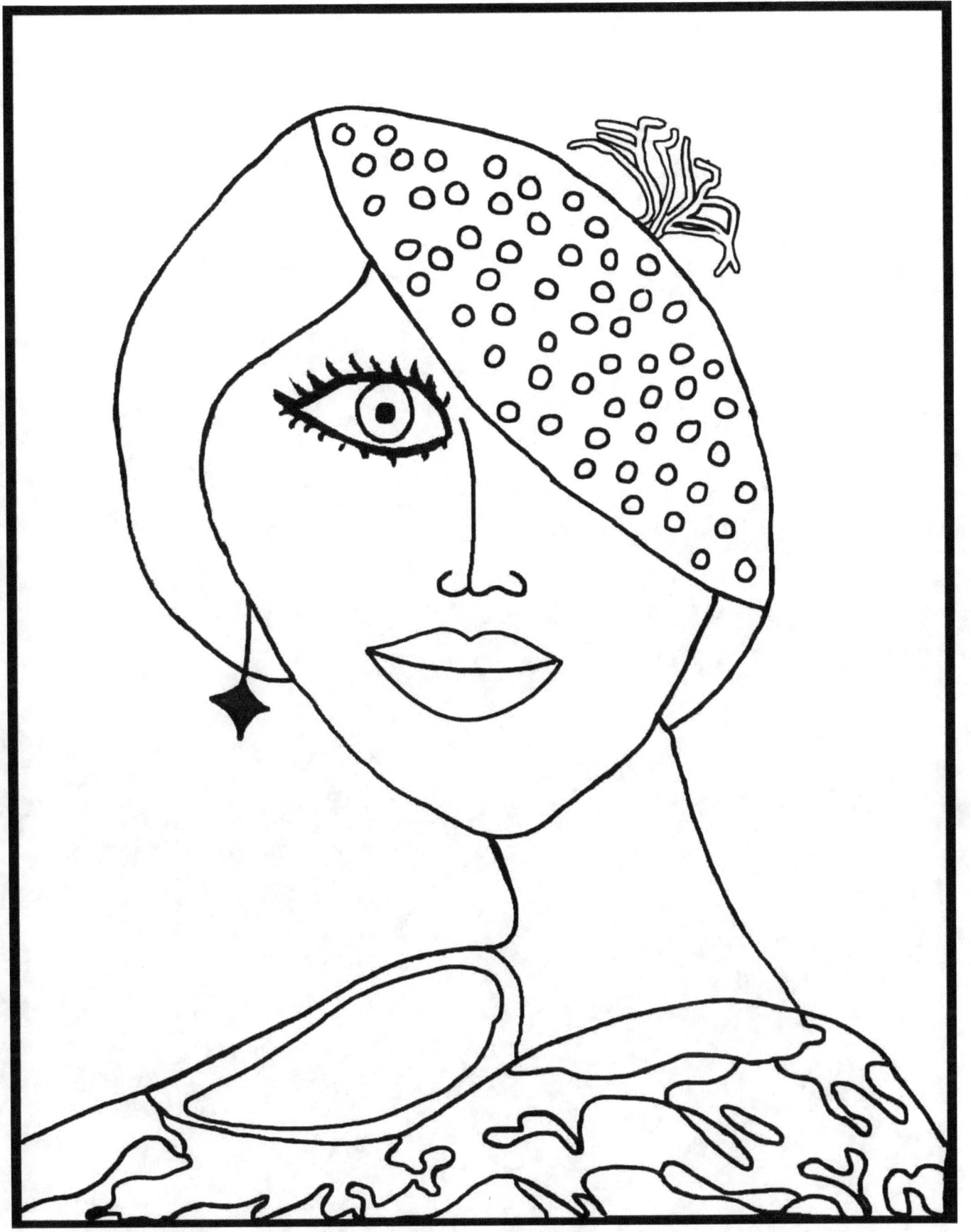

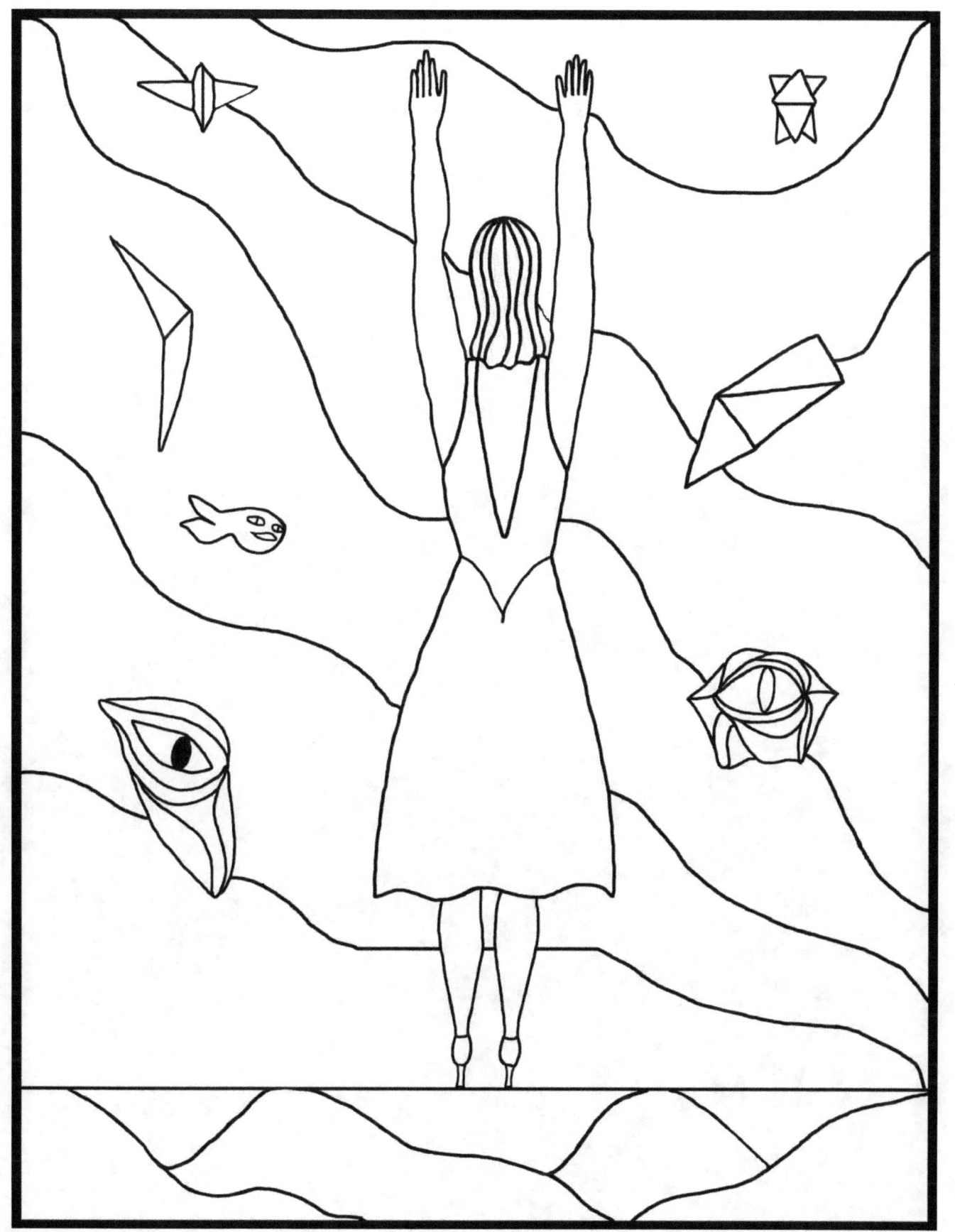

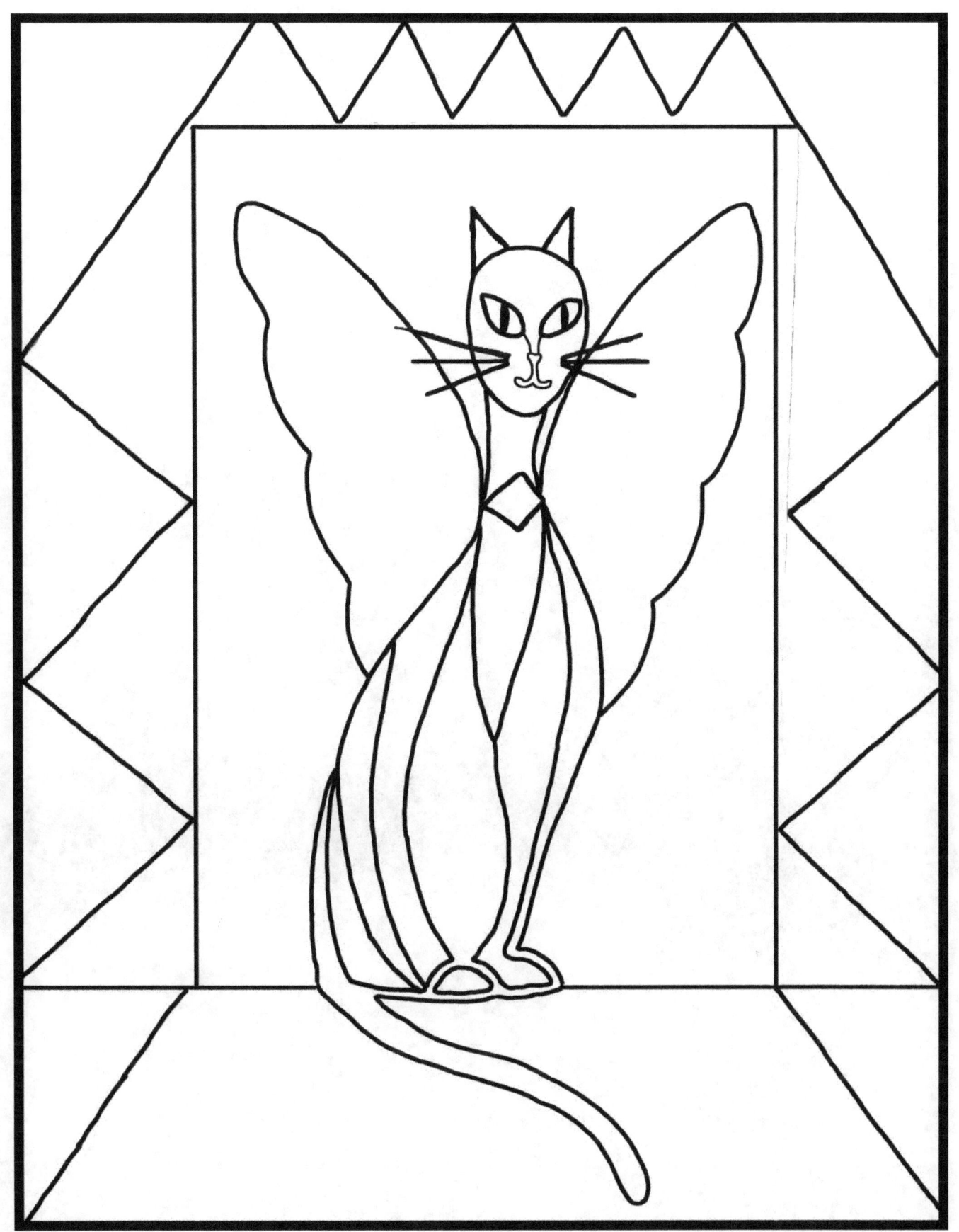

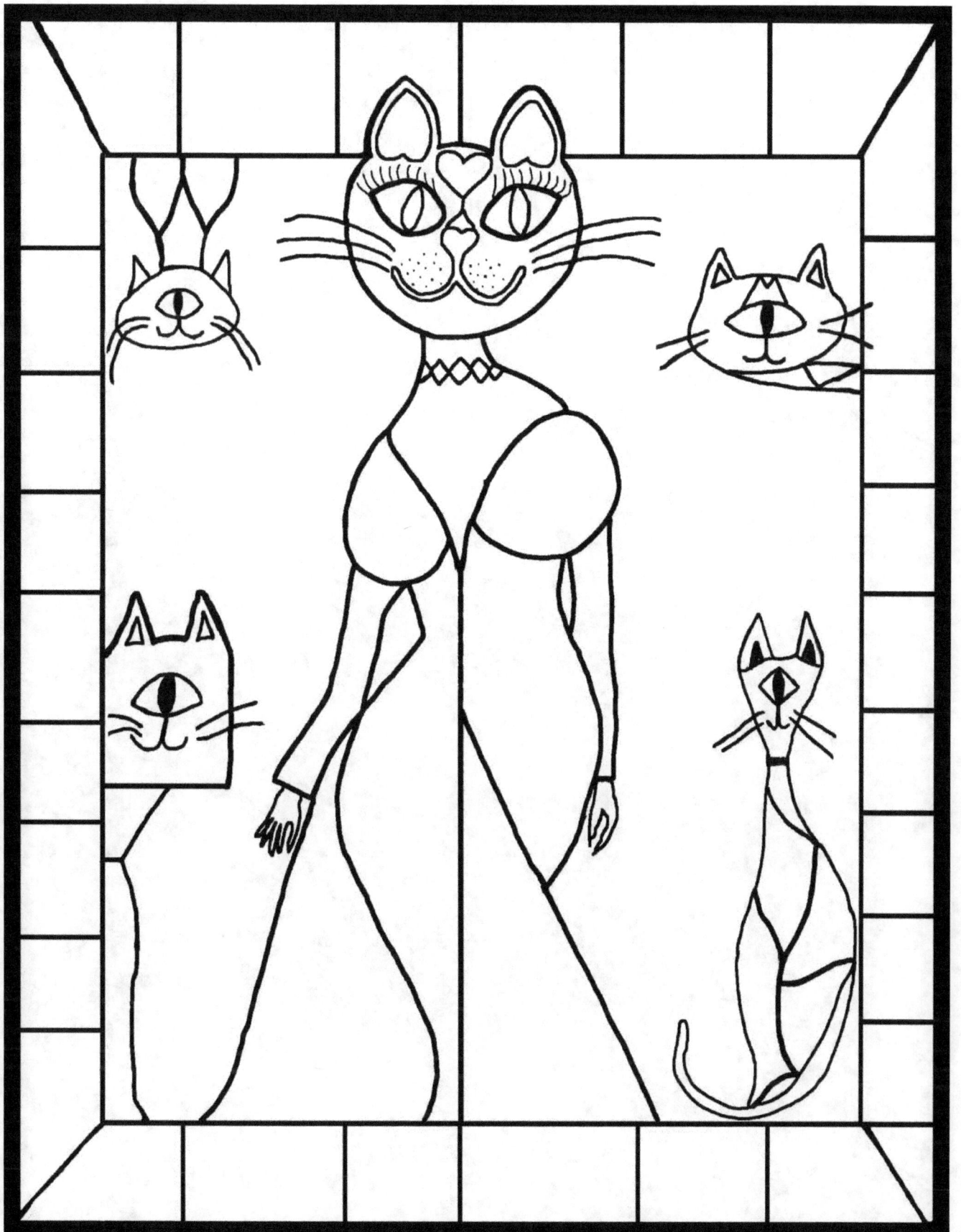

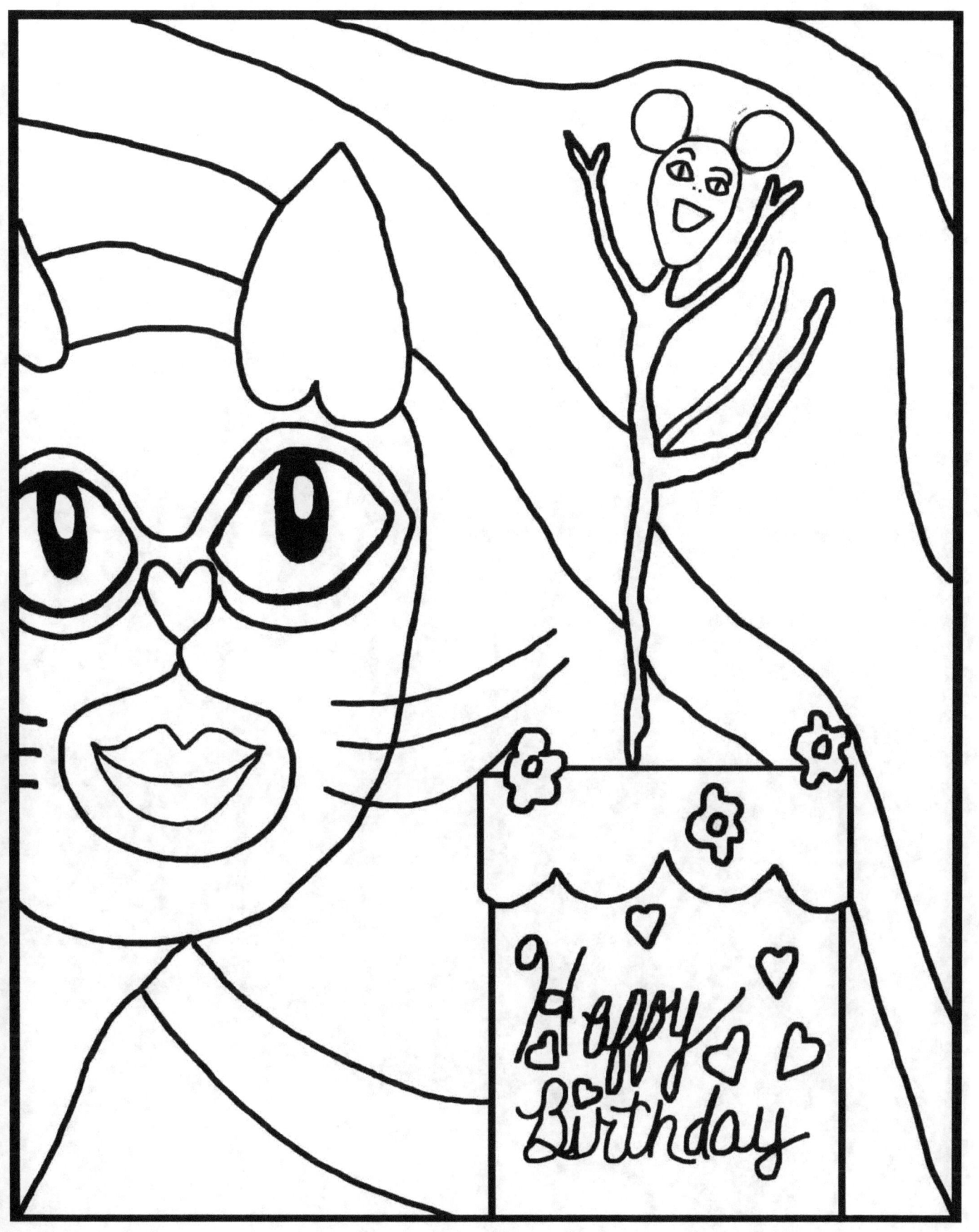

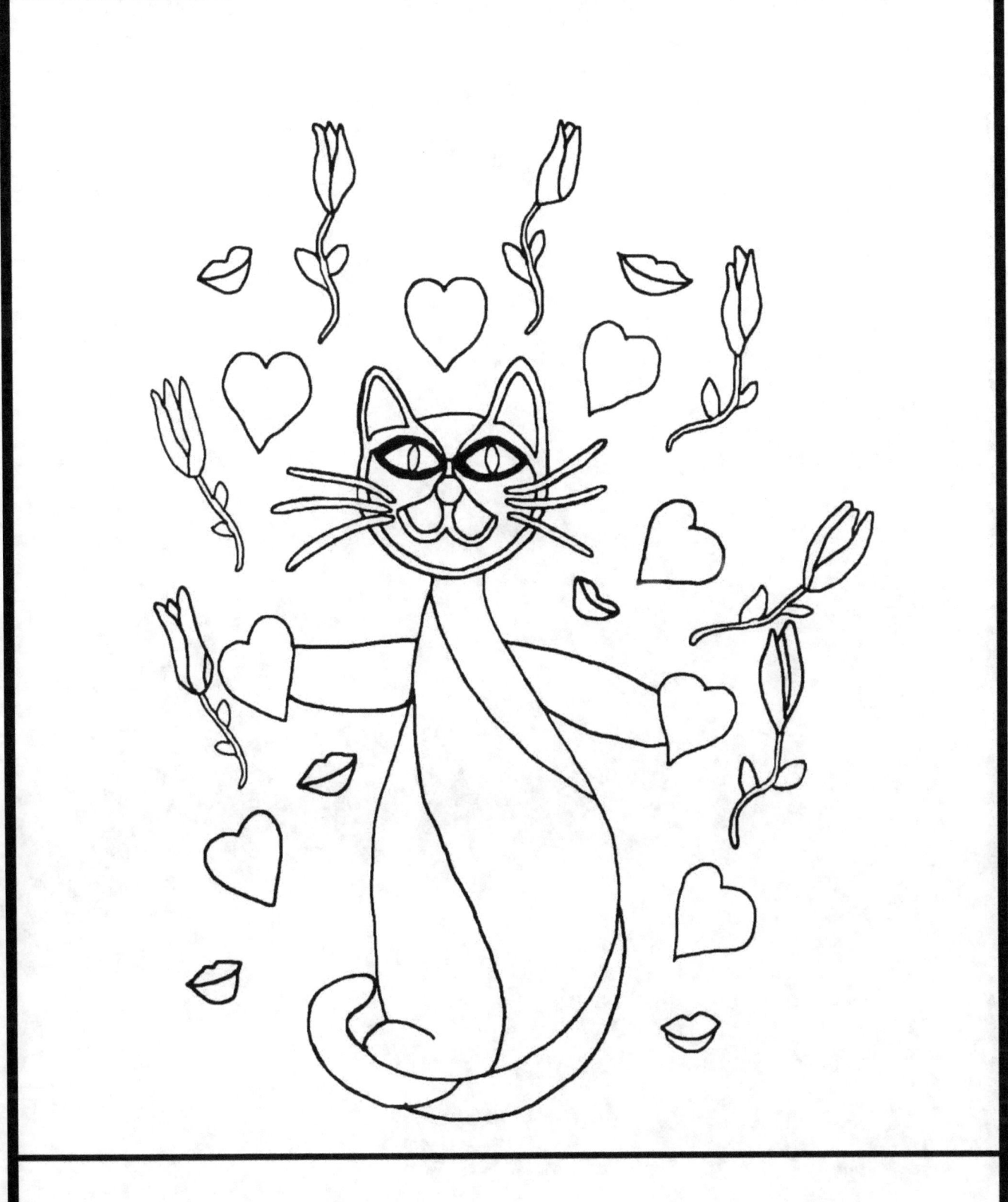

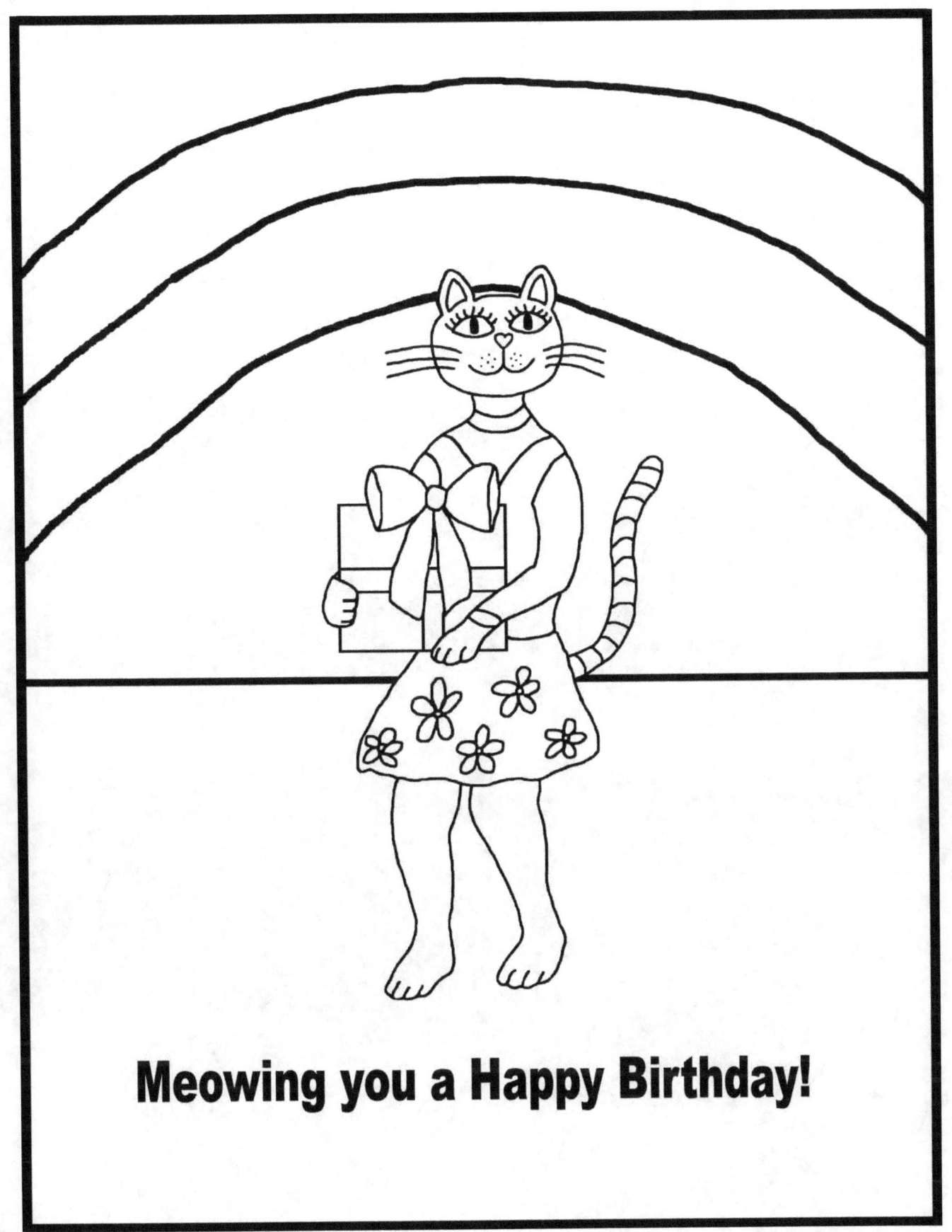

Meowing you a Happy Birthday!

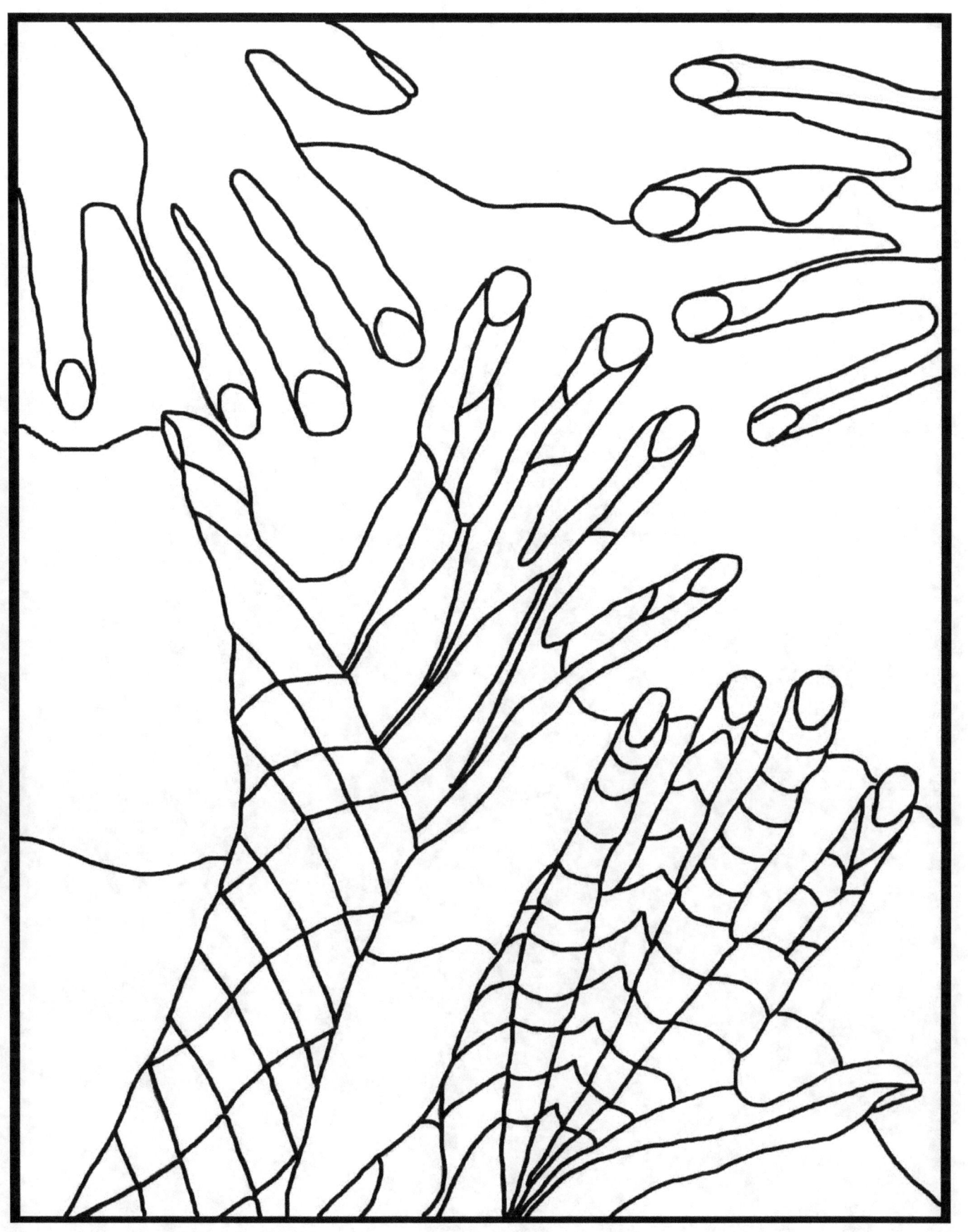

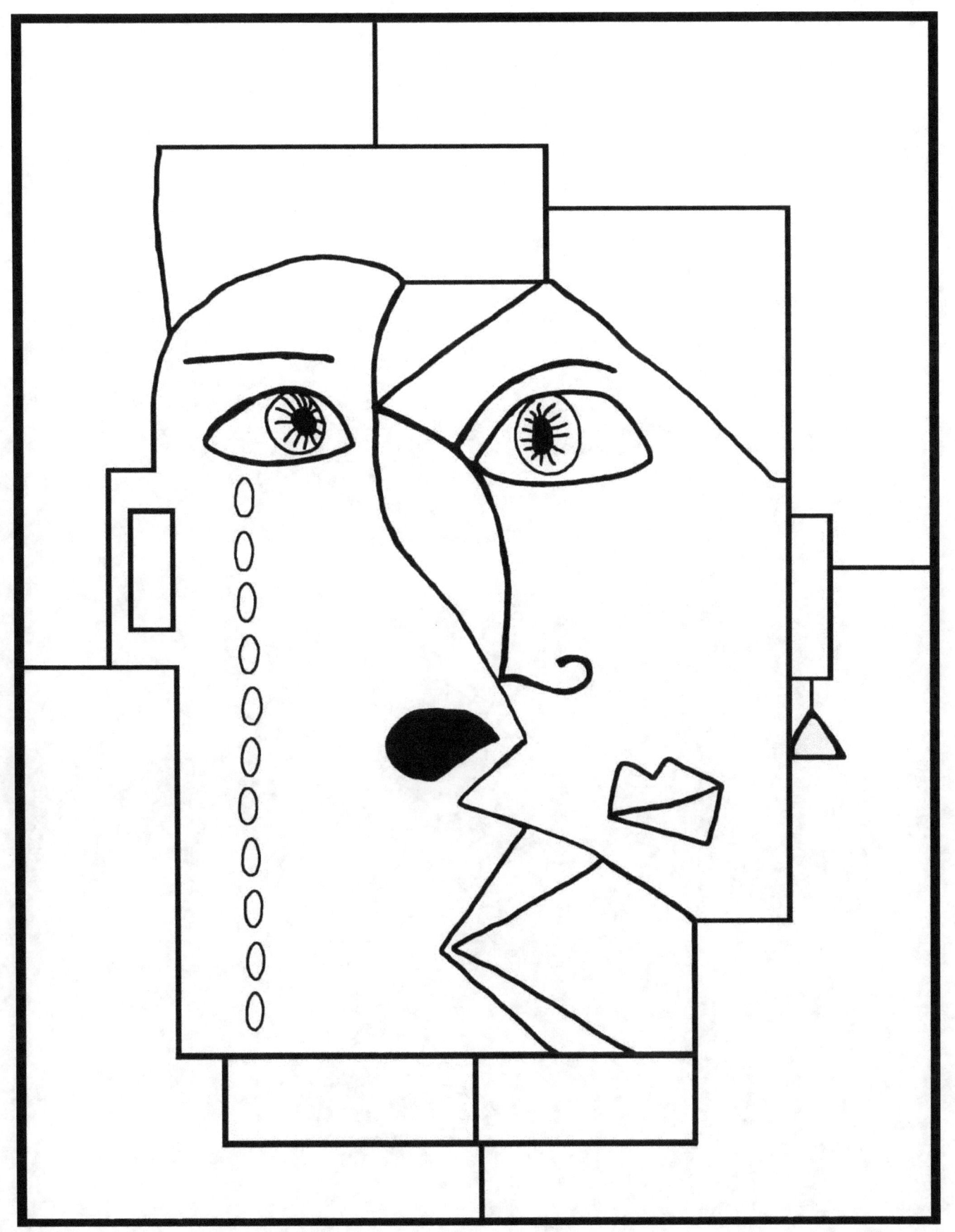

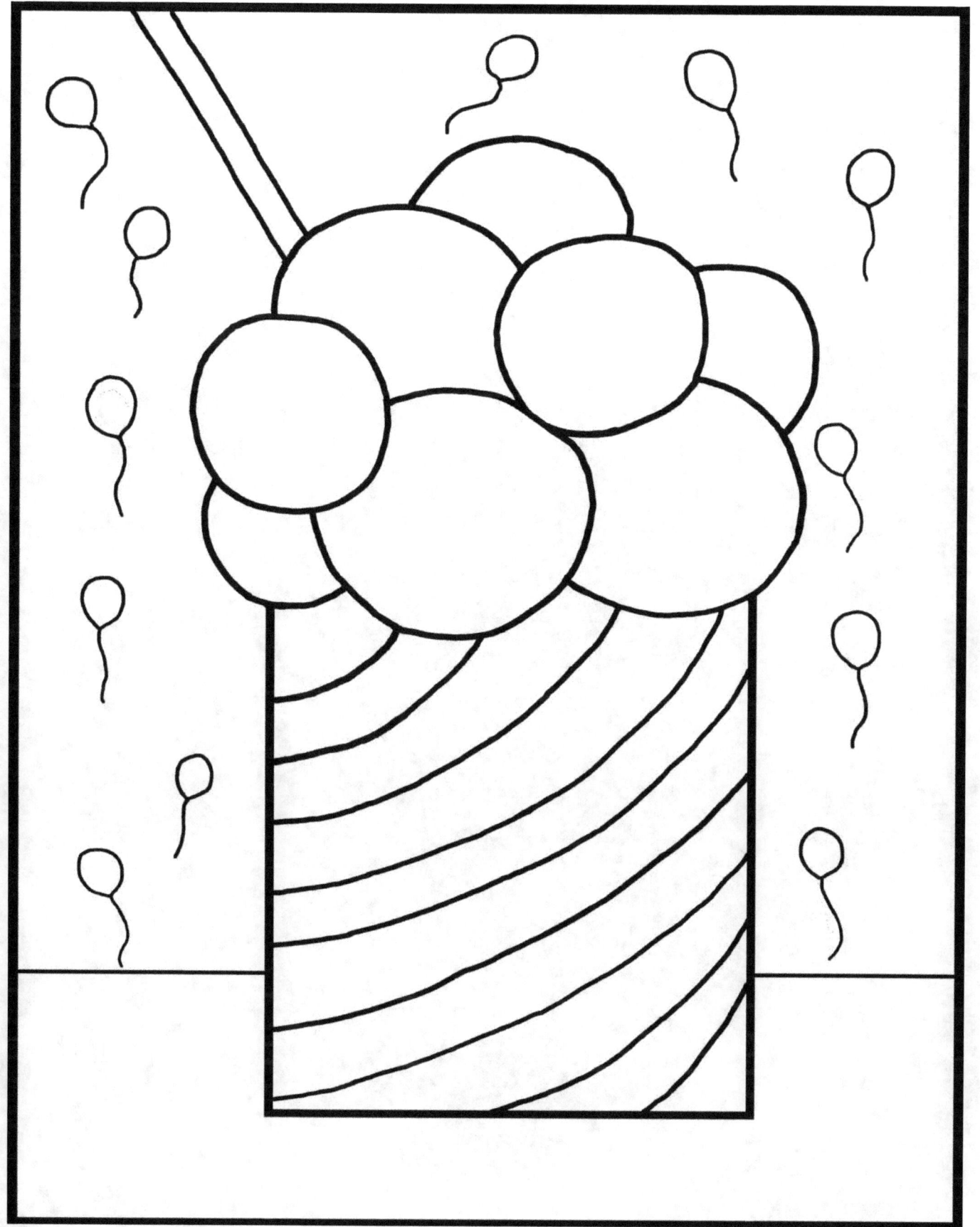

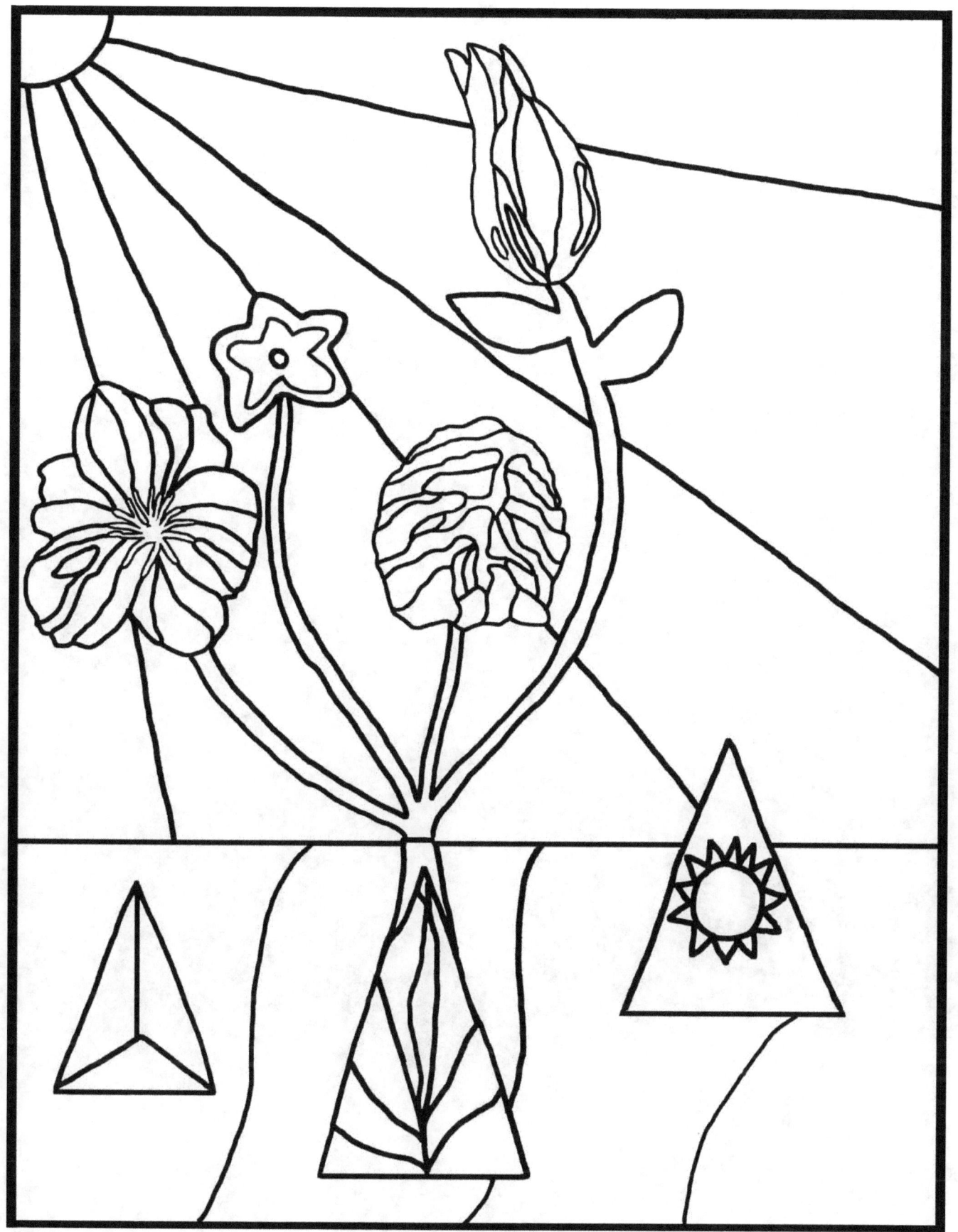

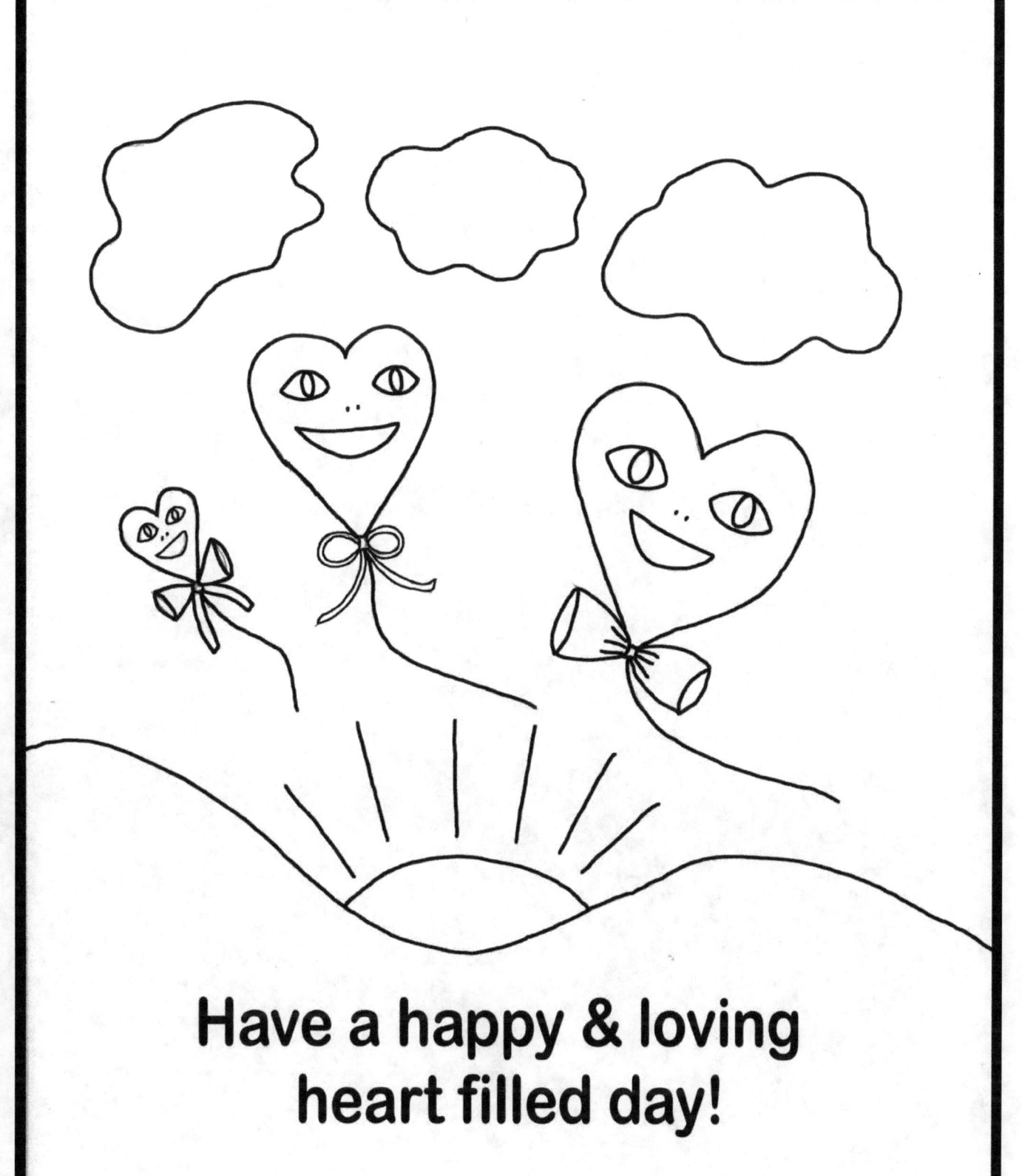

Have a happy & loving heart filled day!

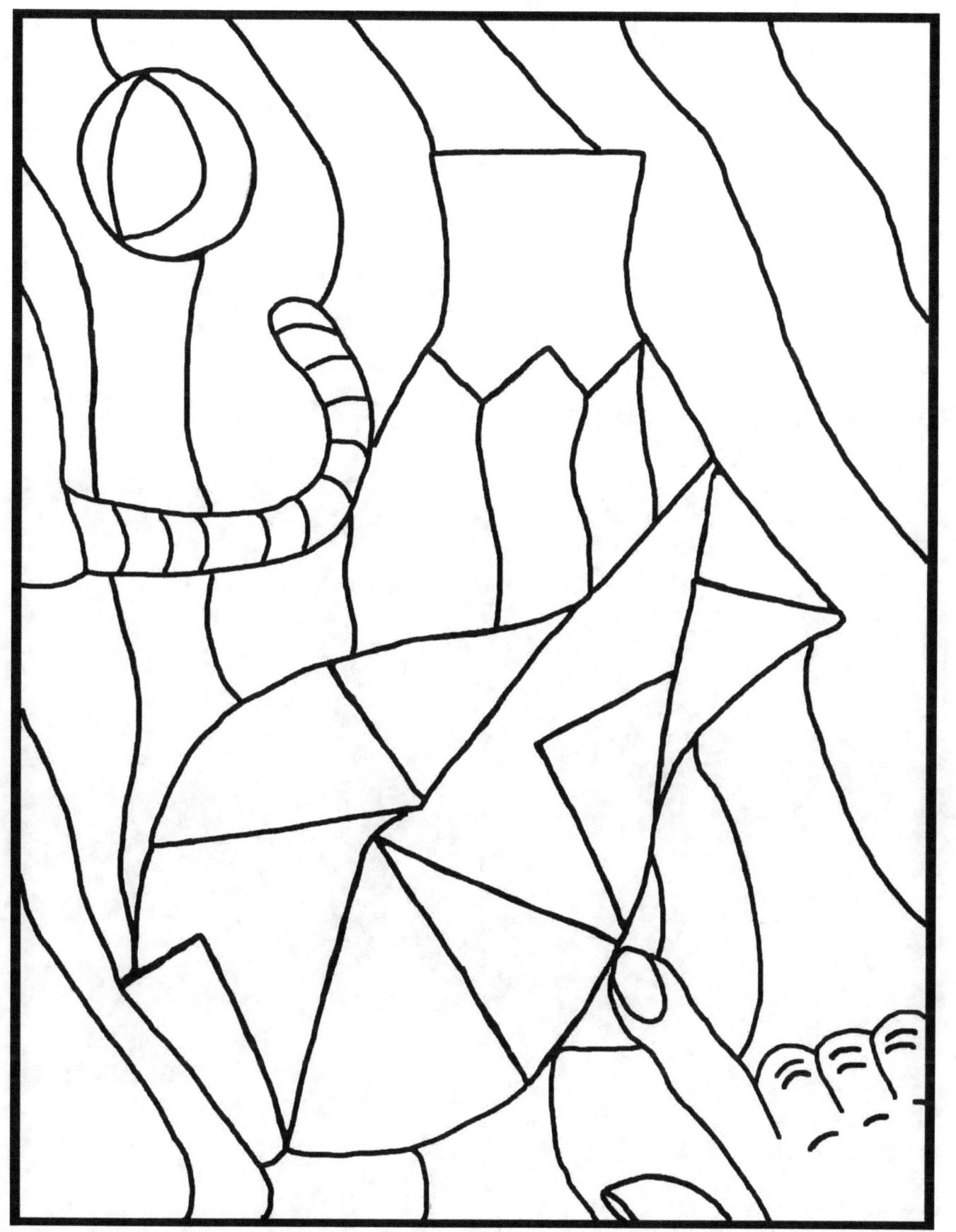

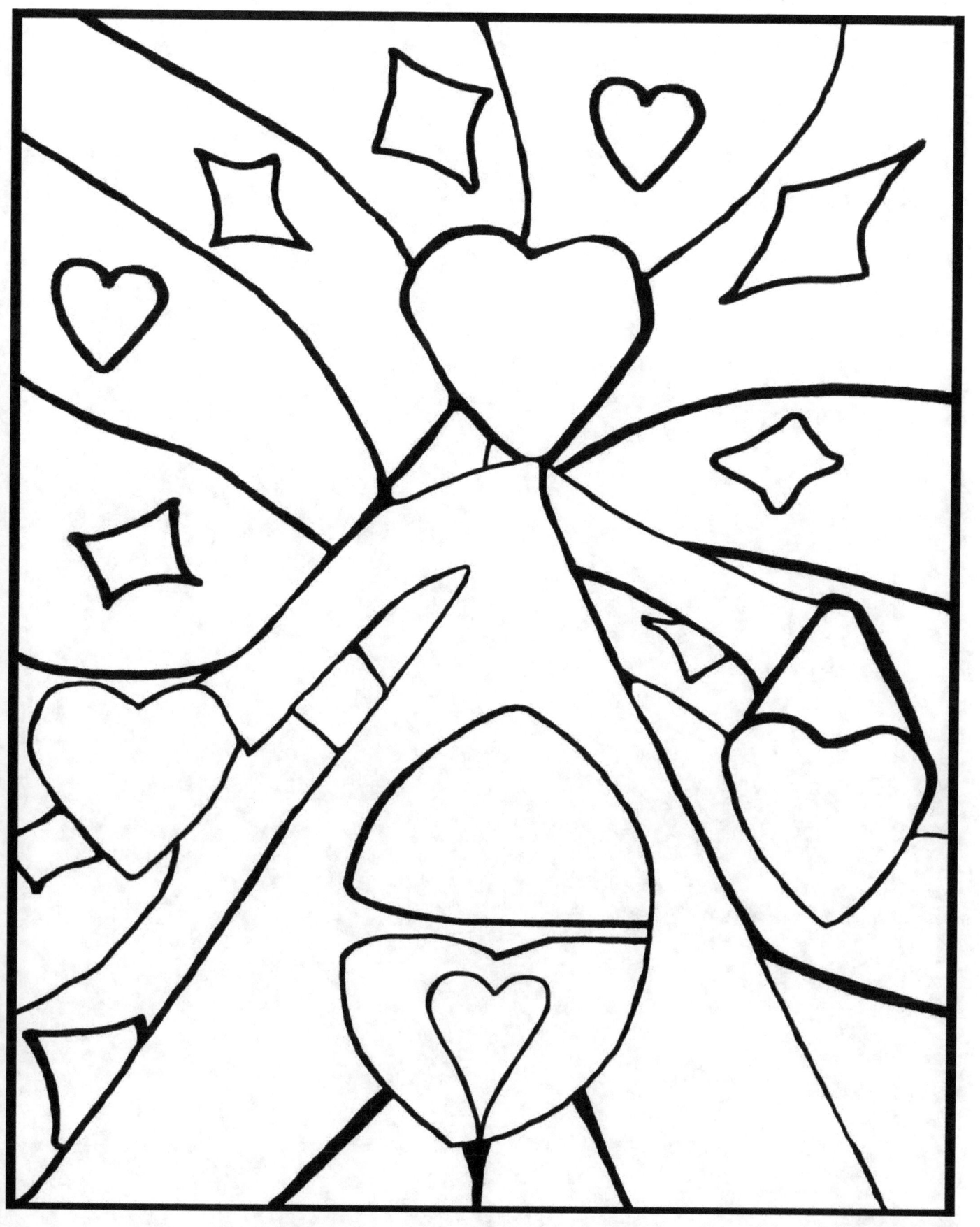

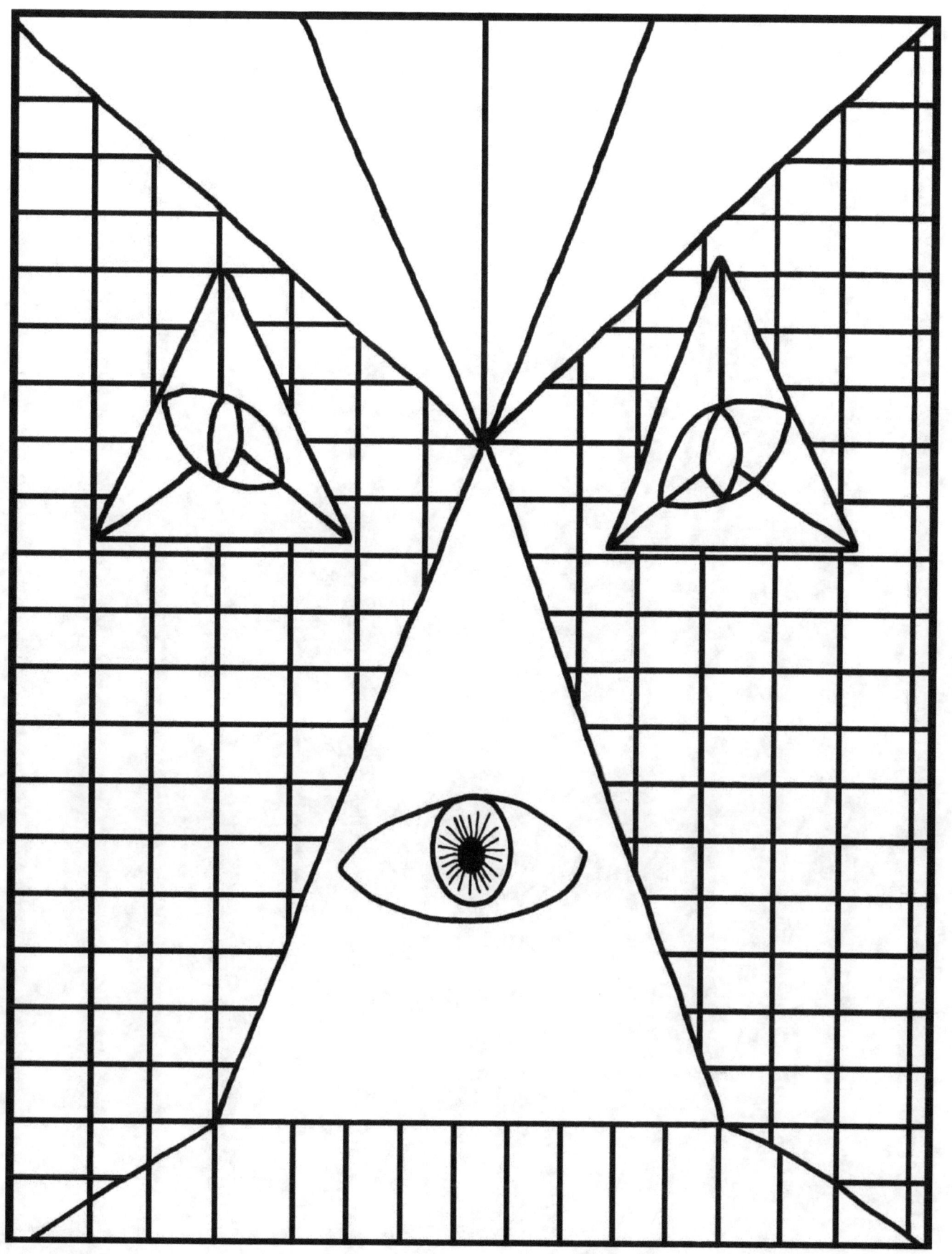

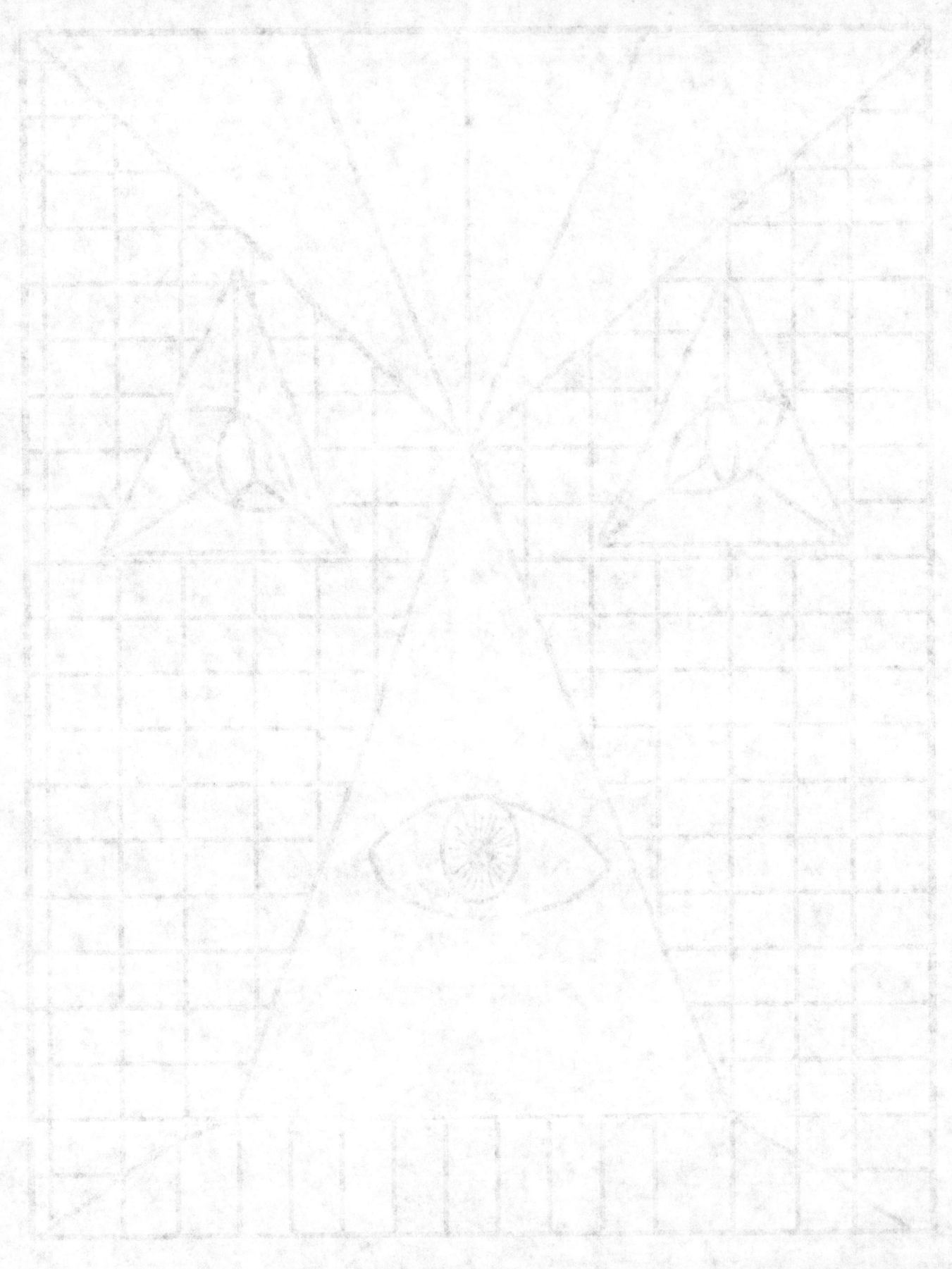

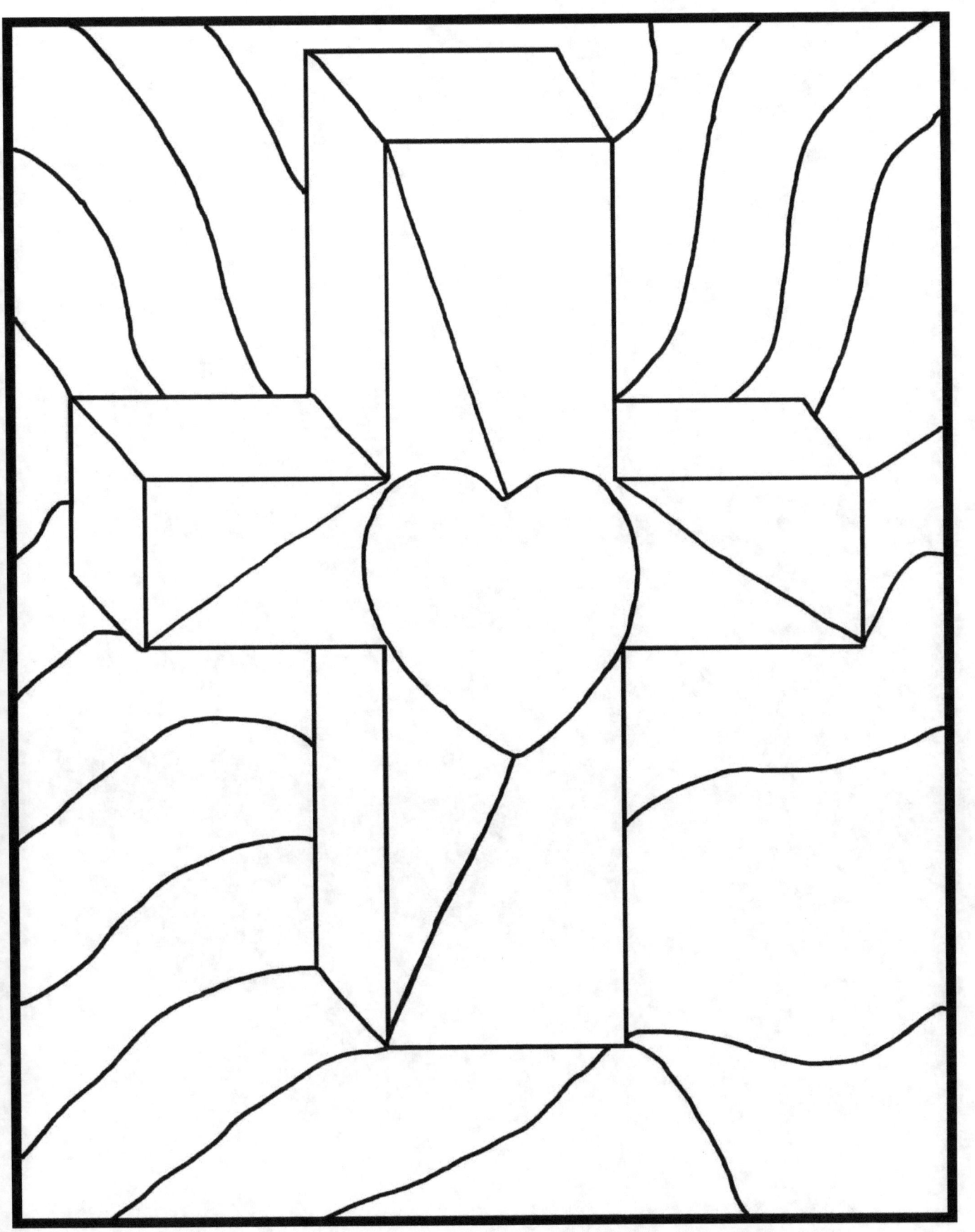

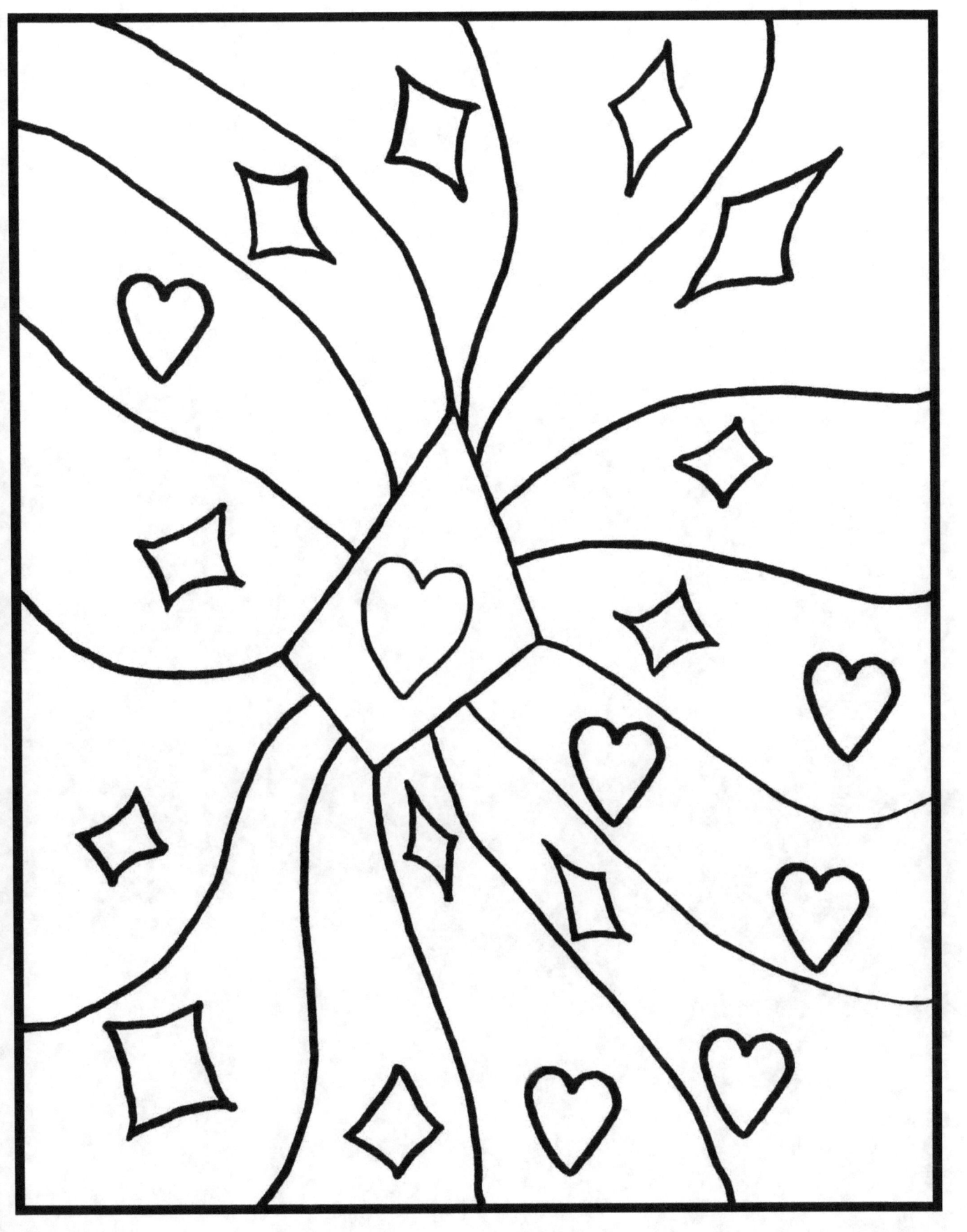

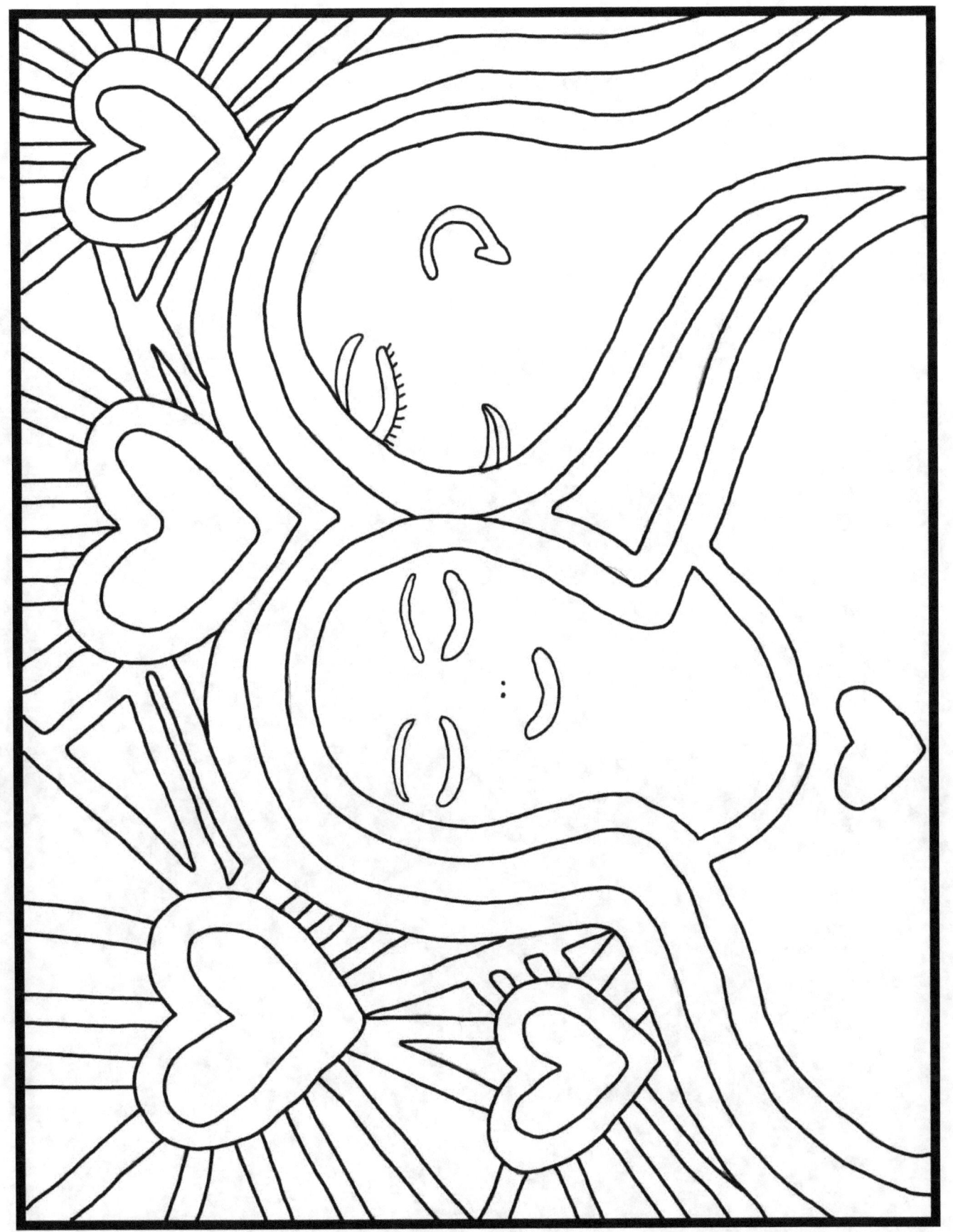

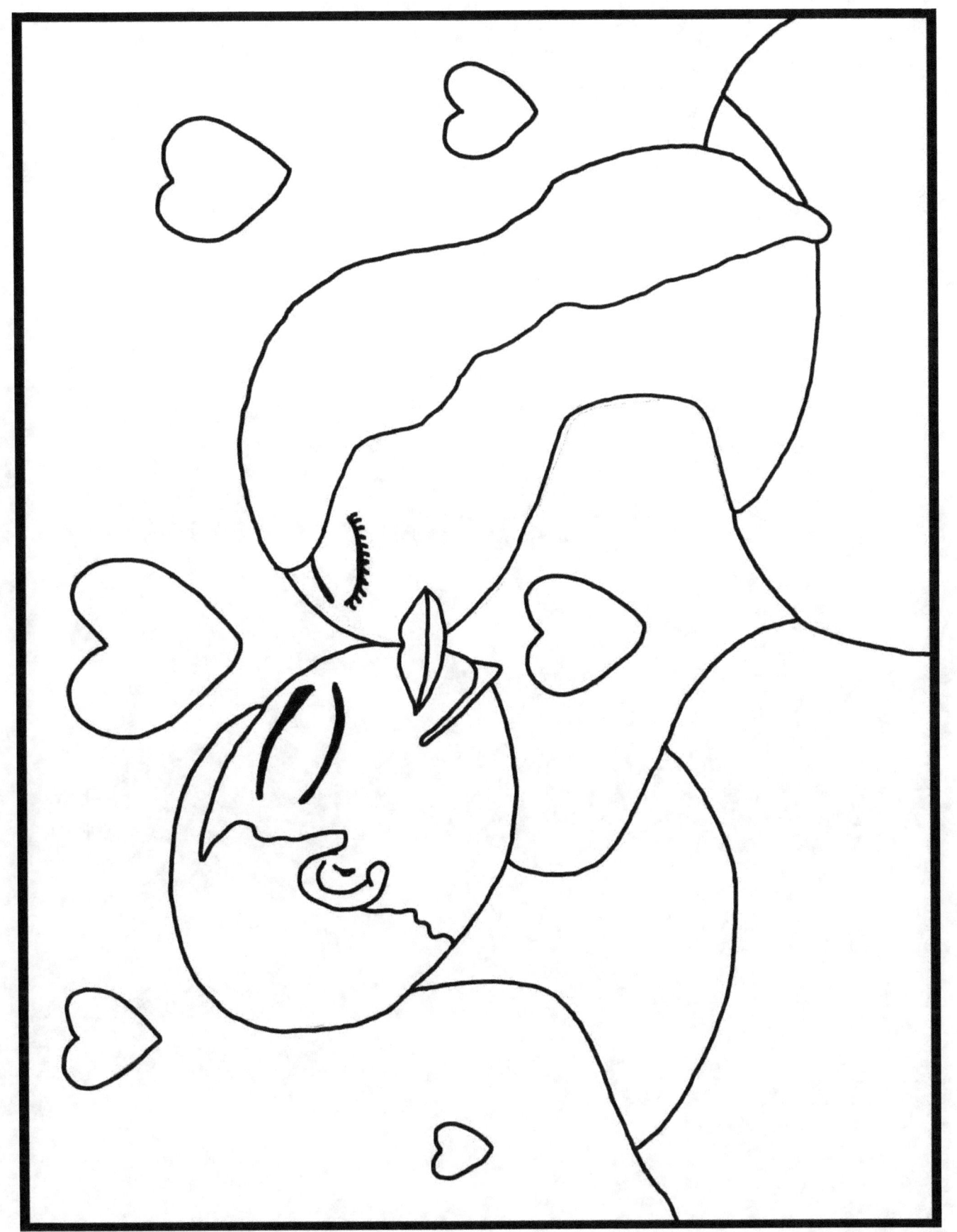

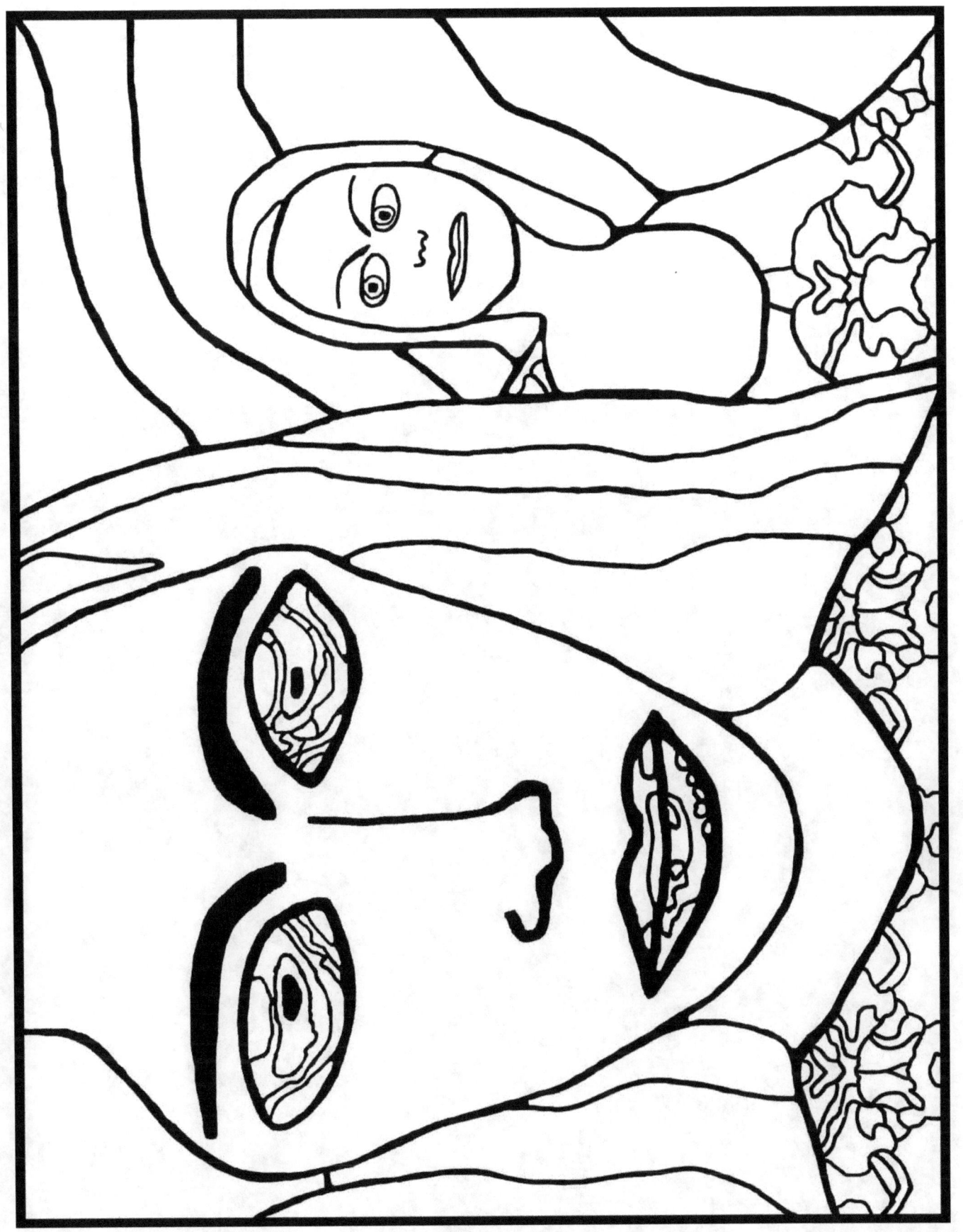

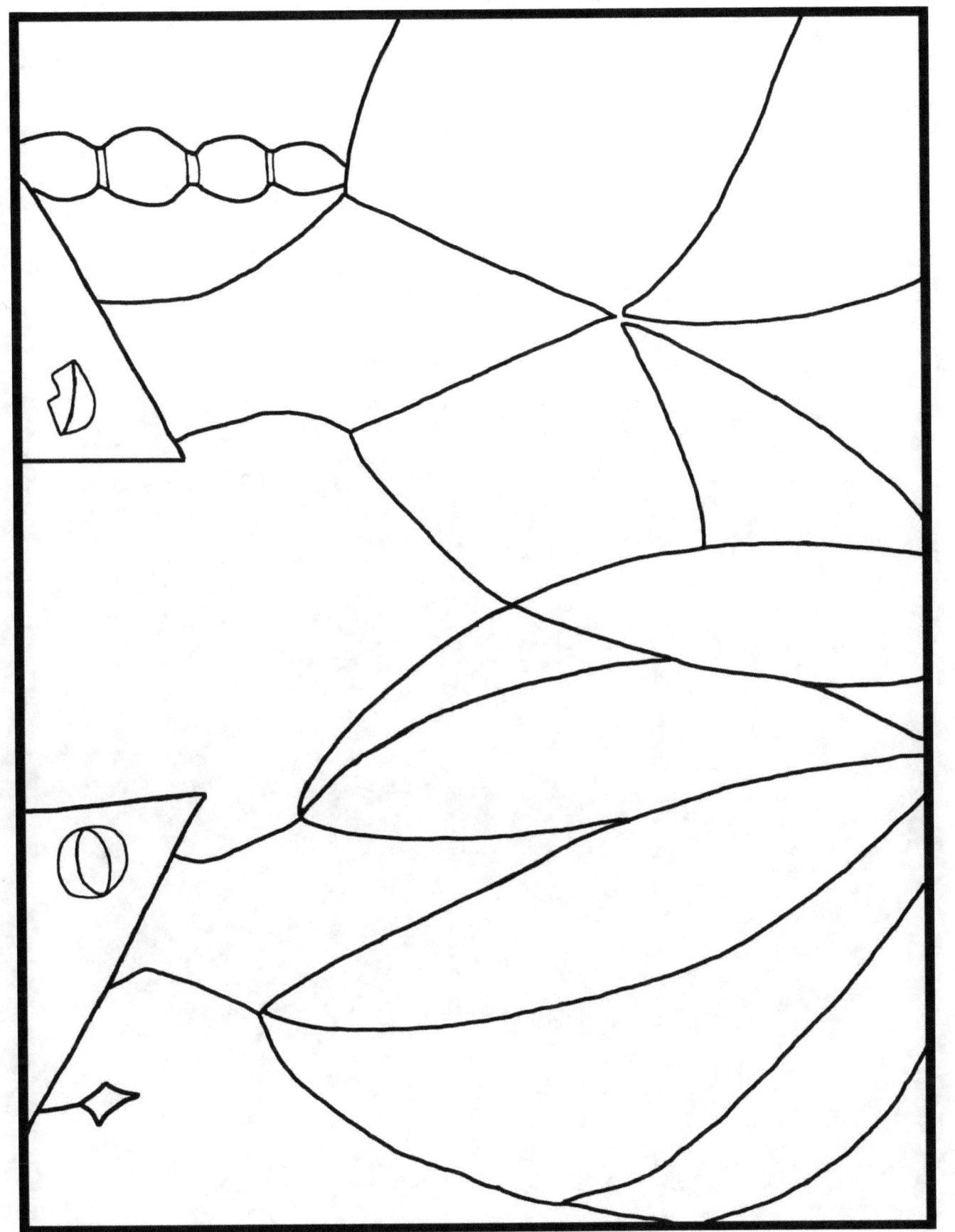

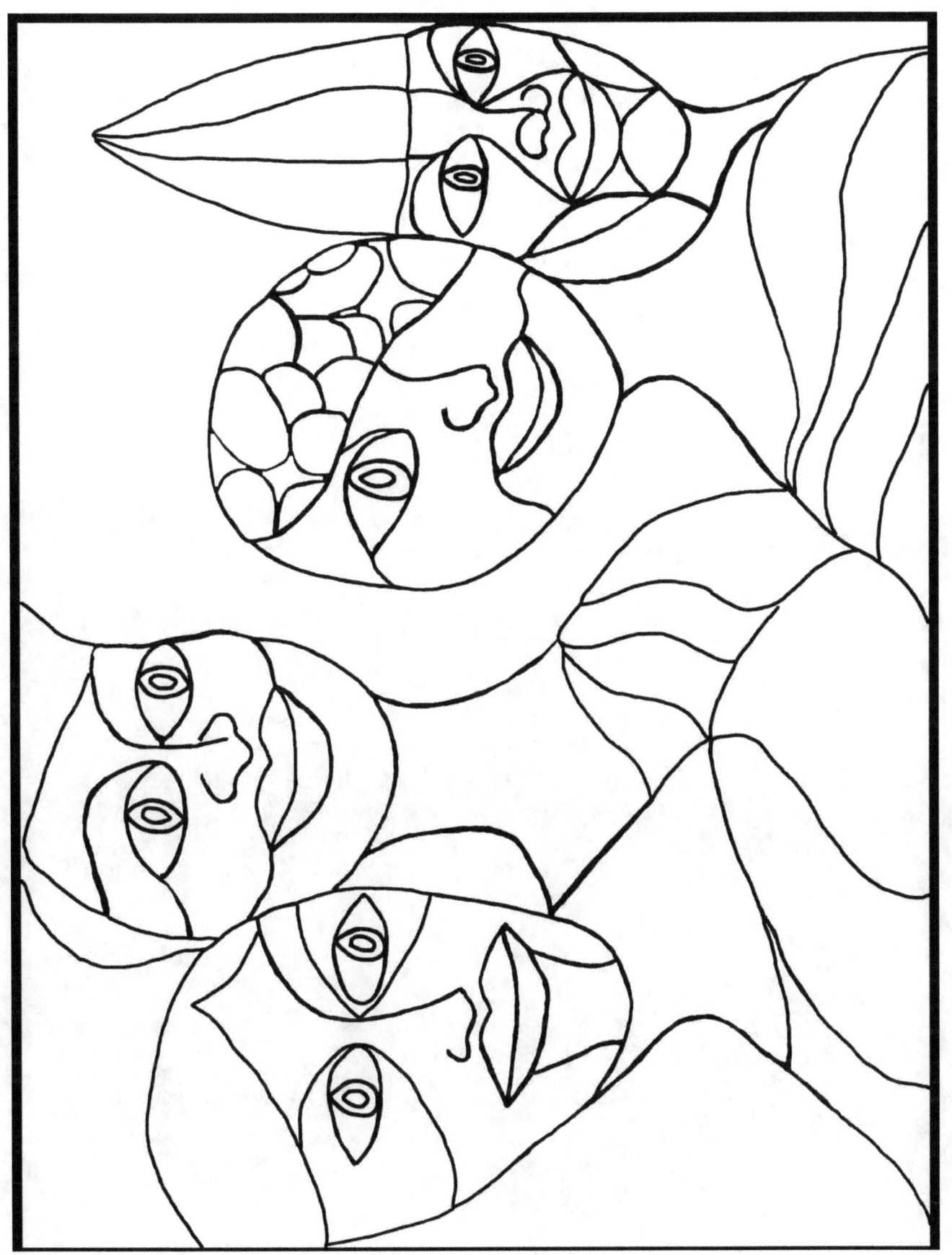

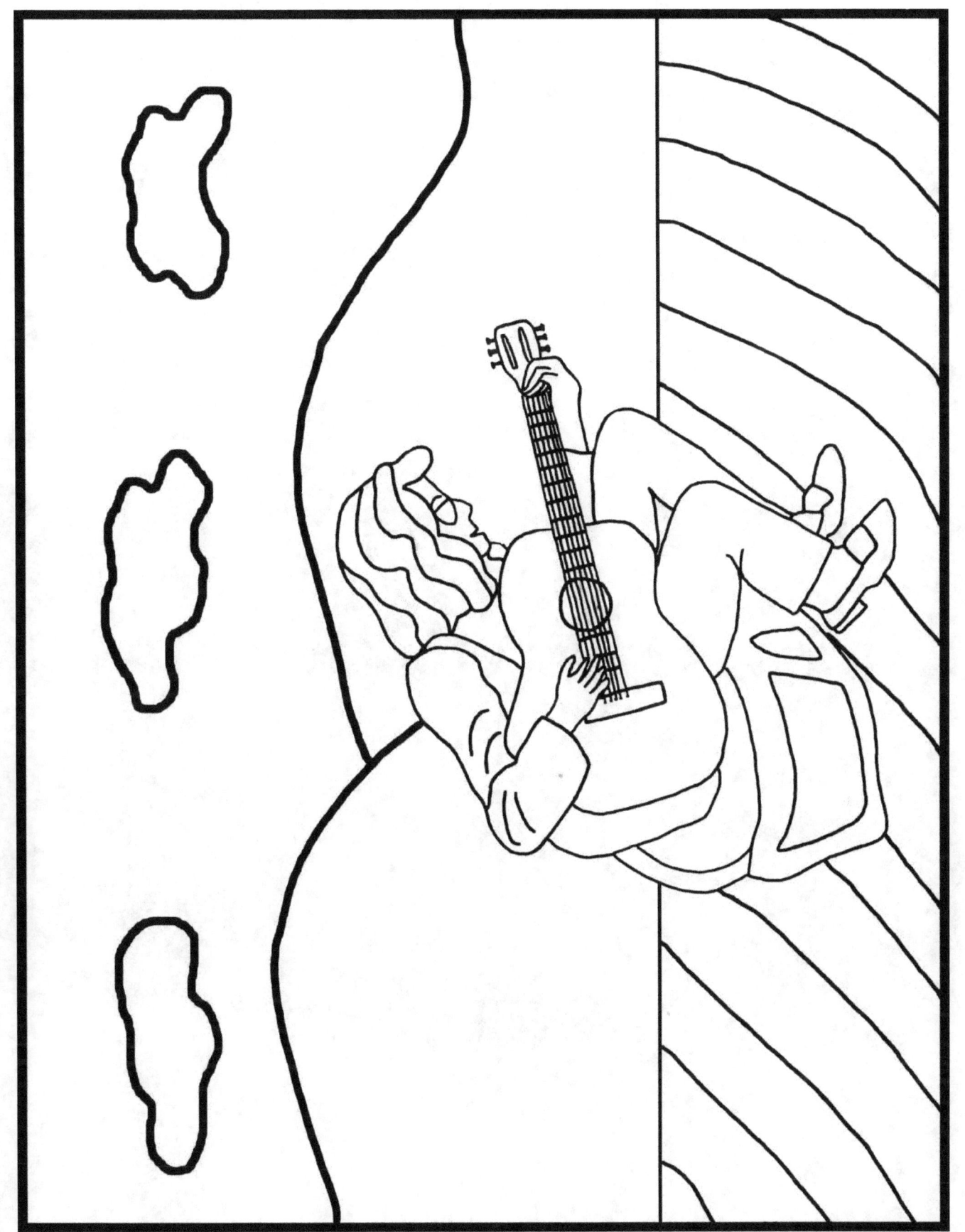

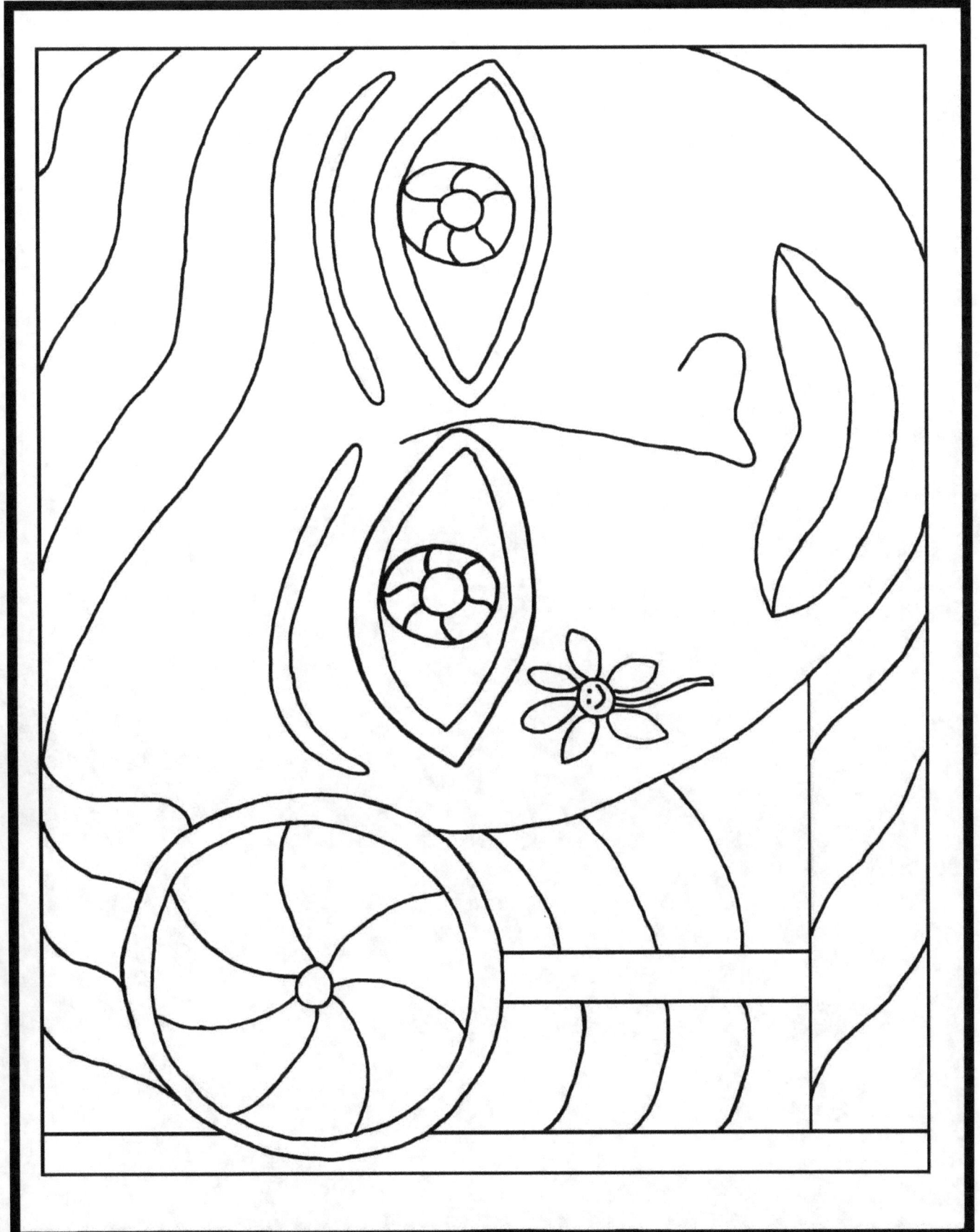

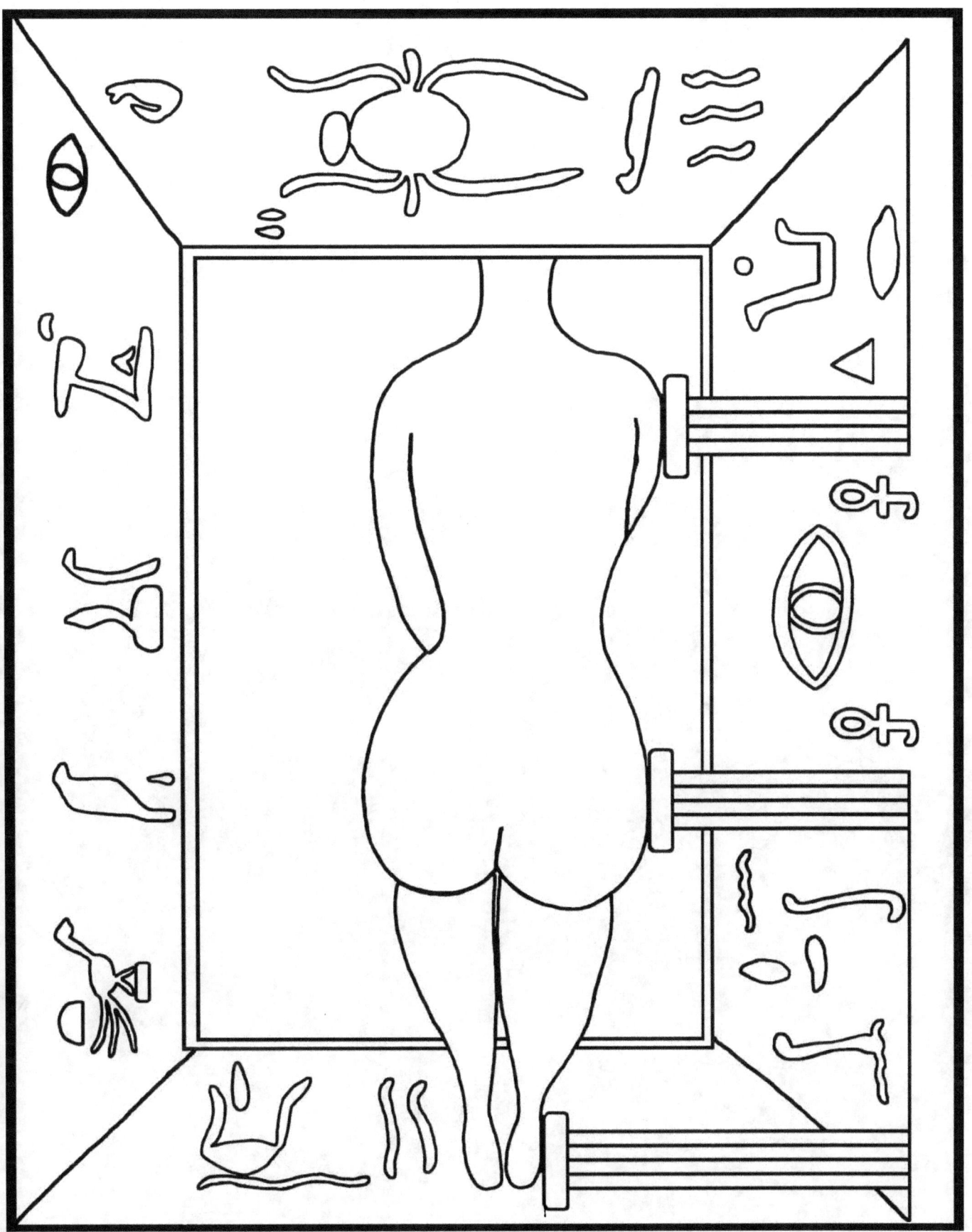

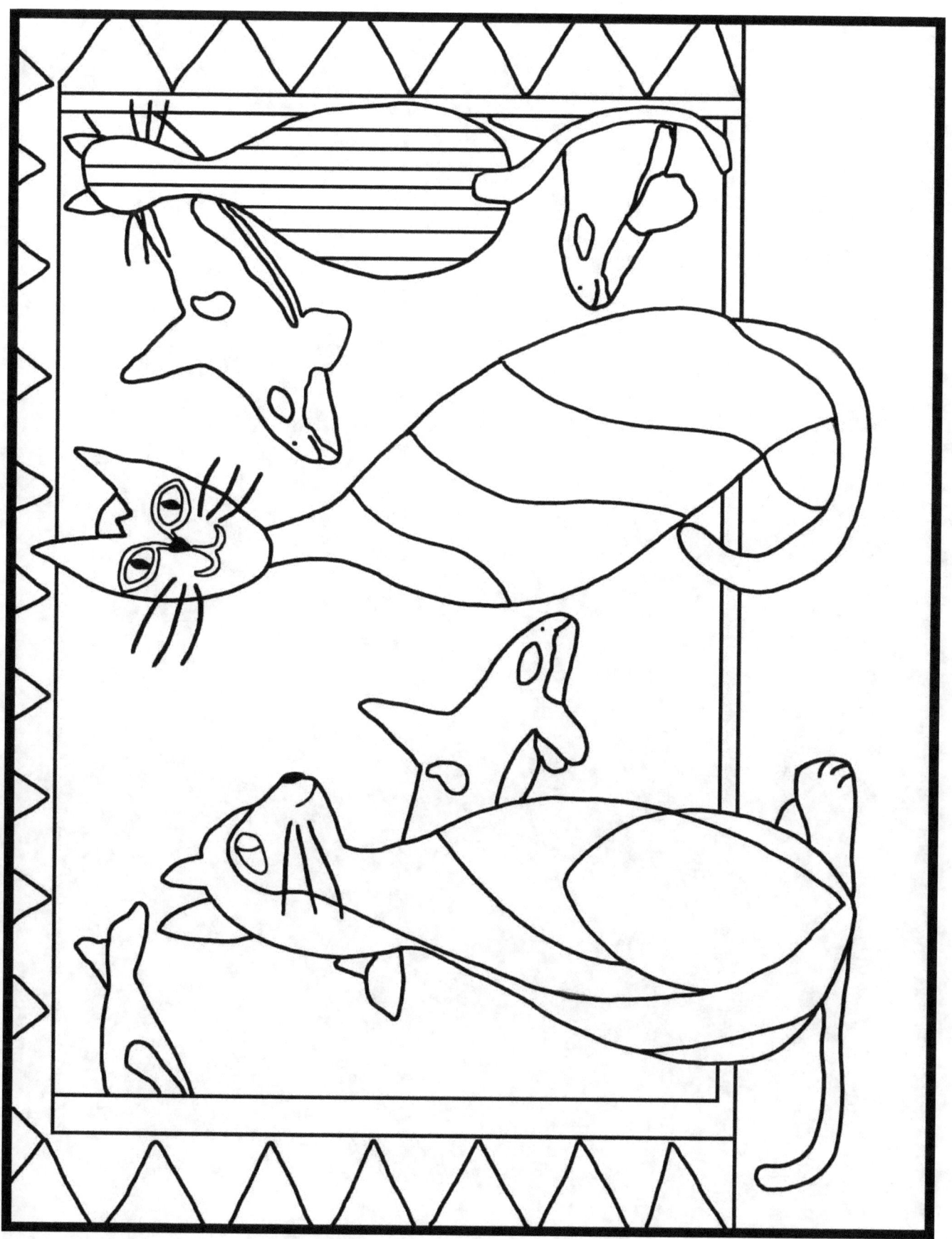

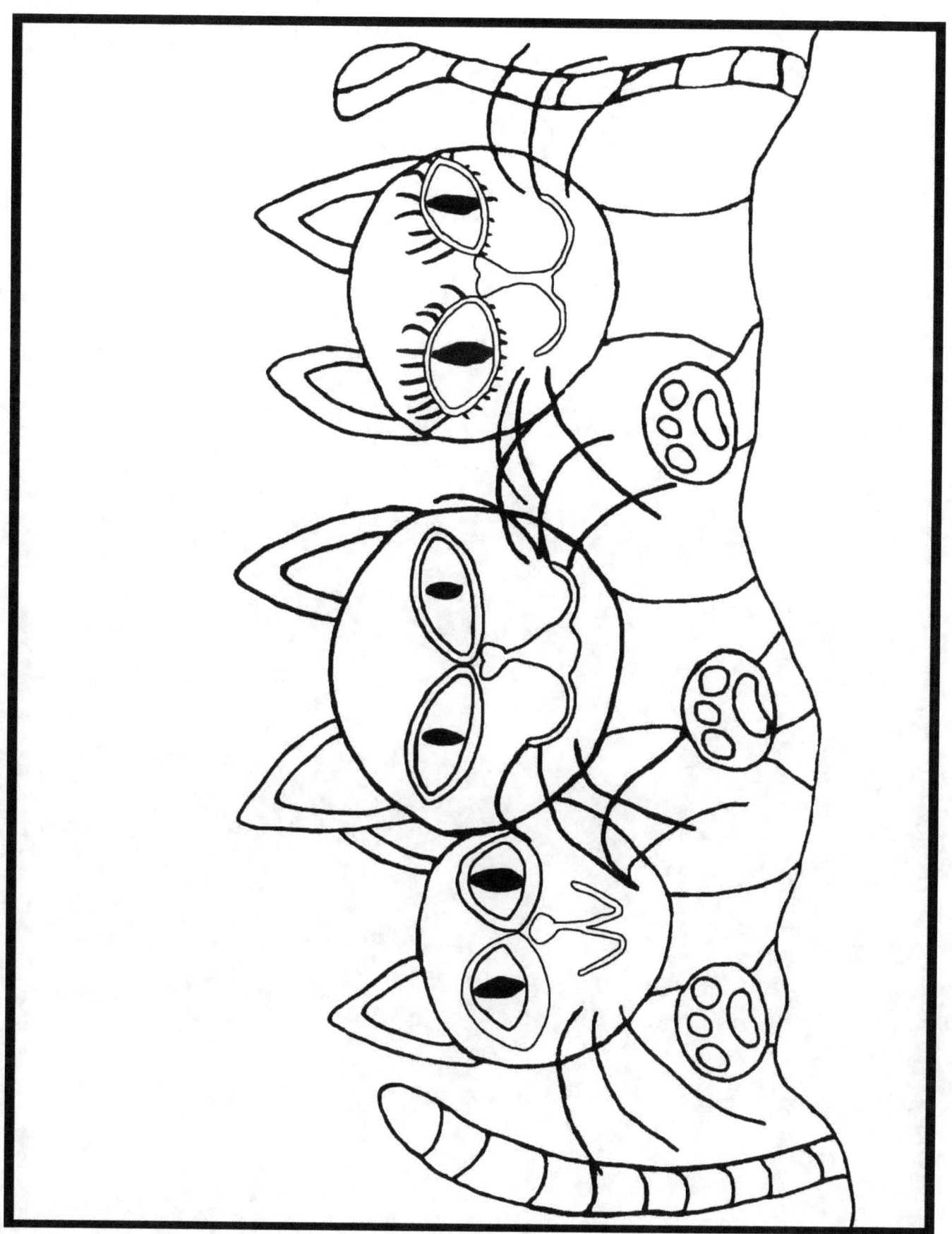

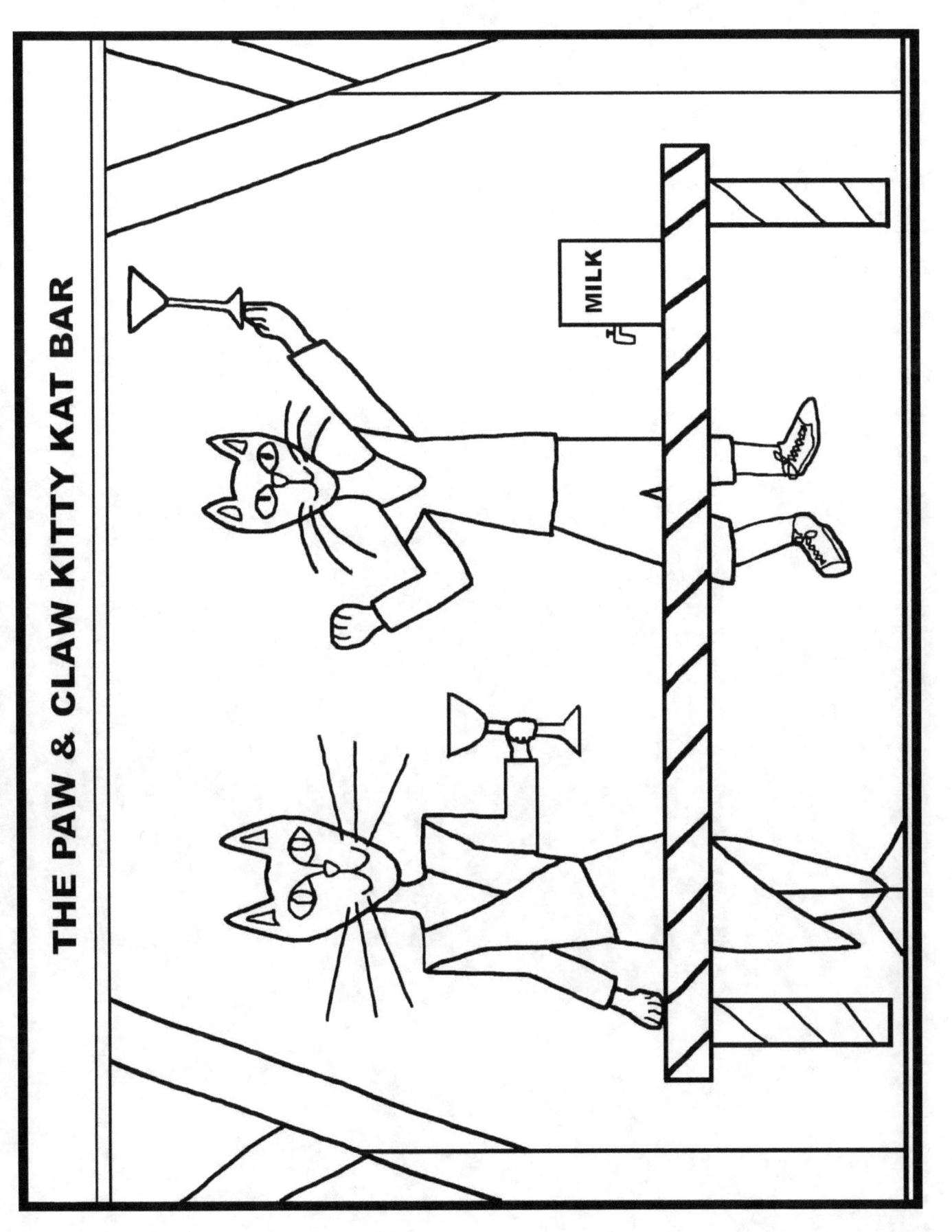

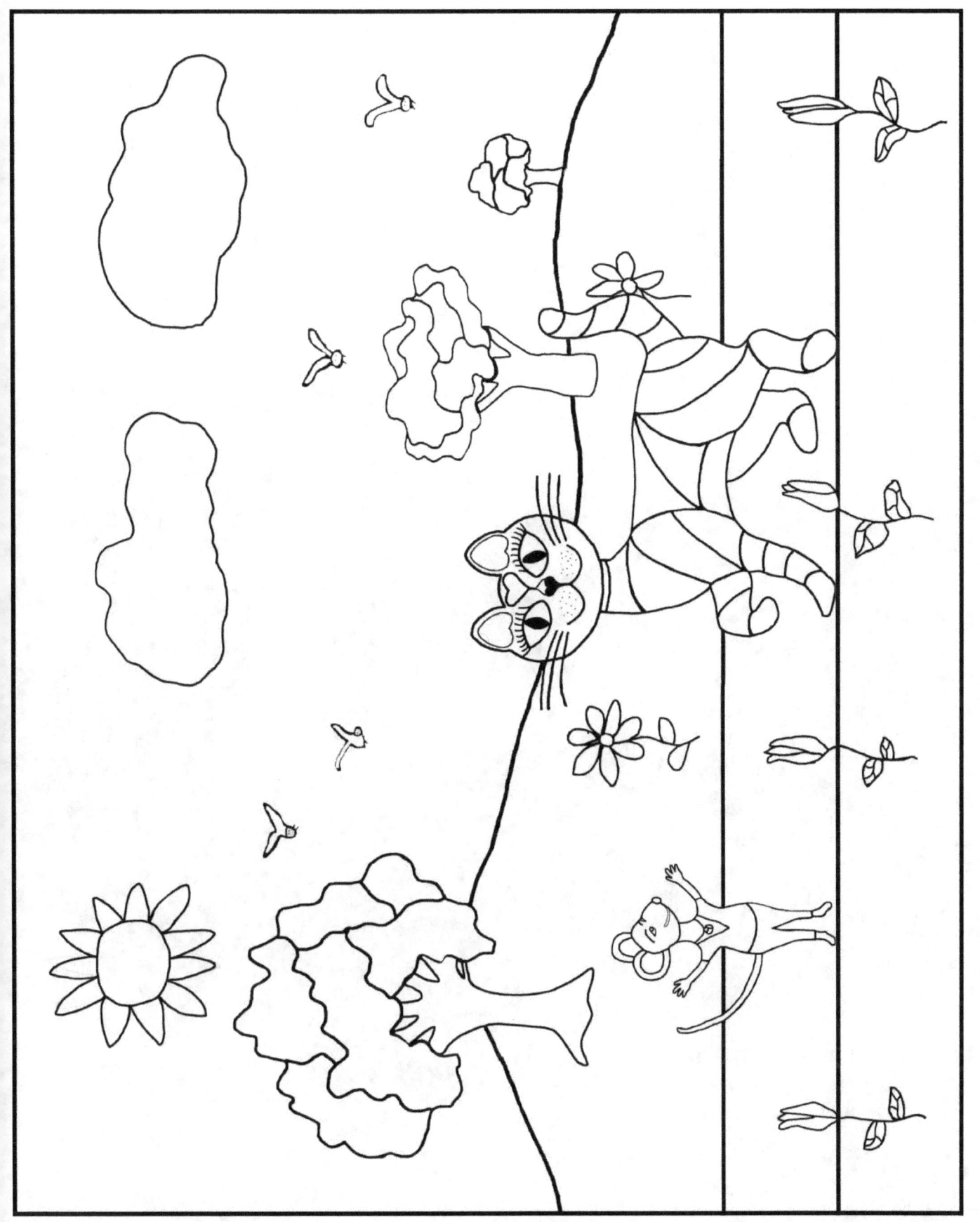

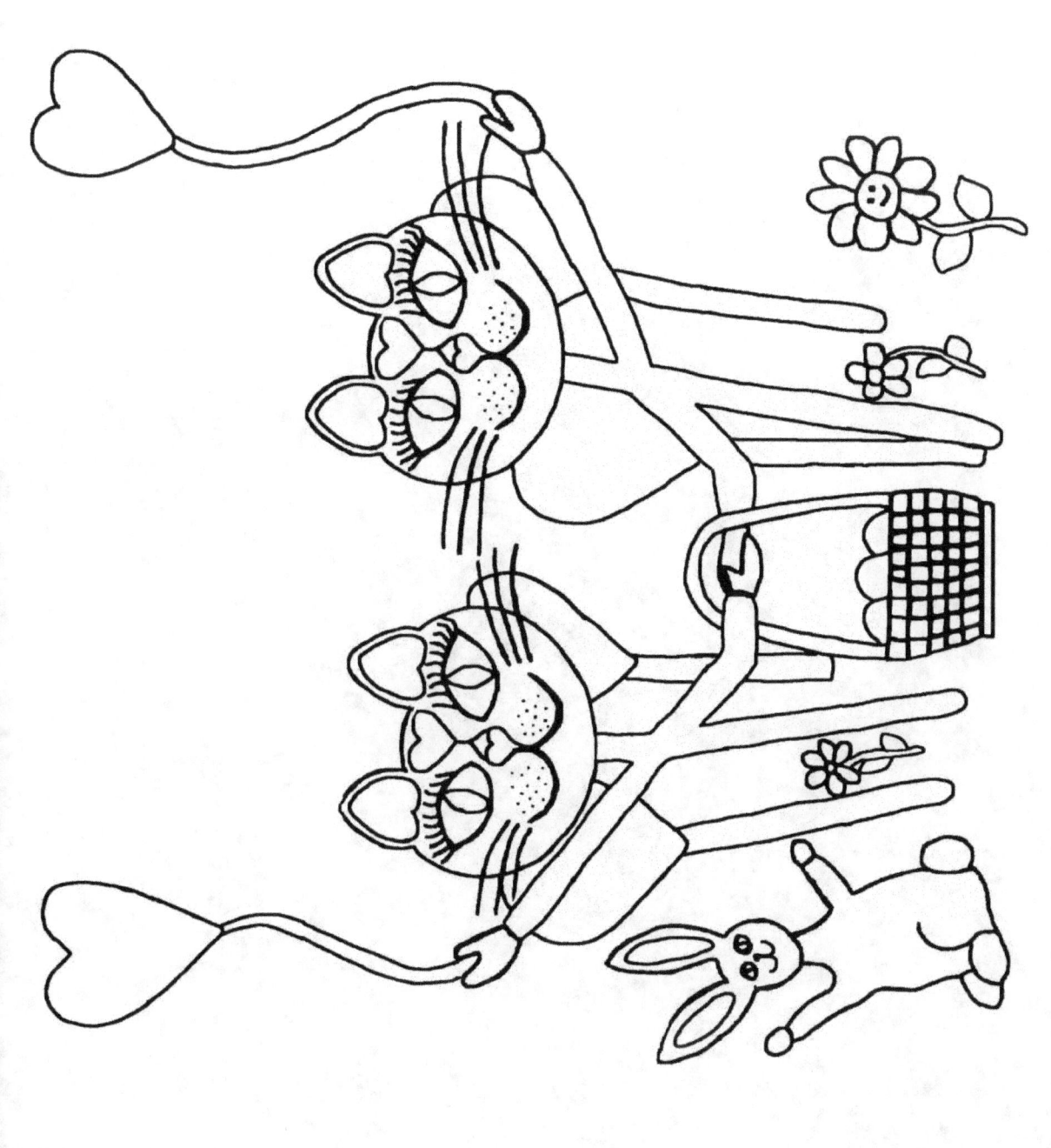

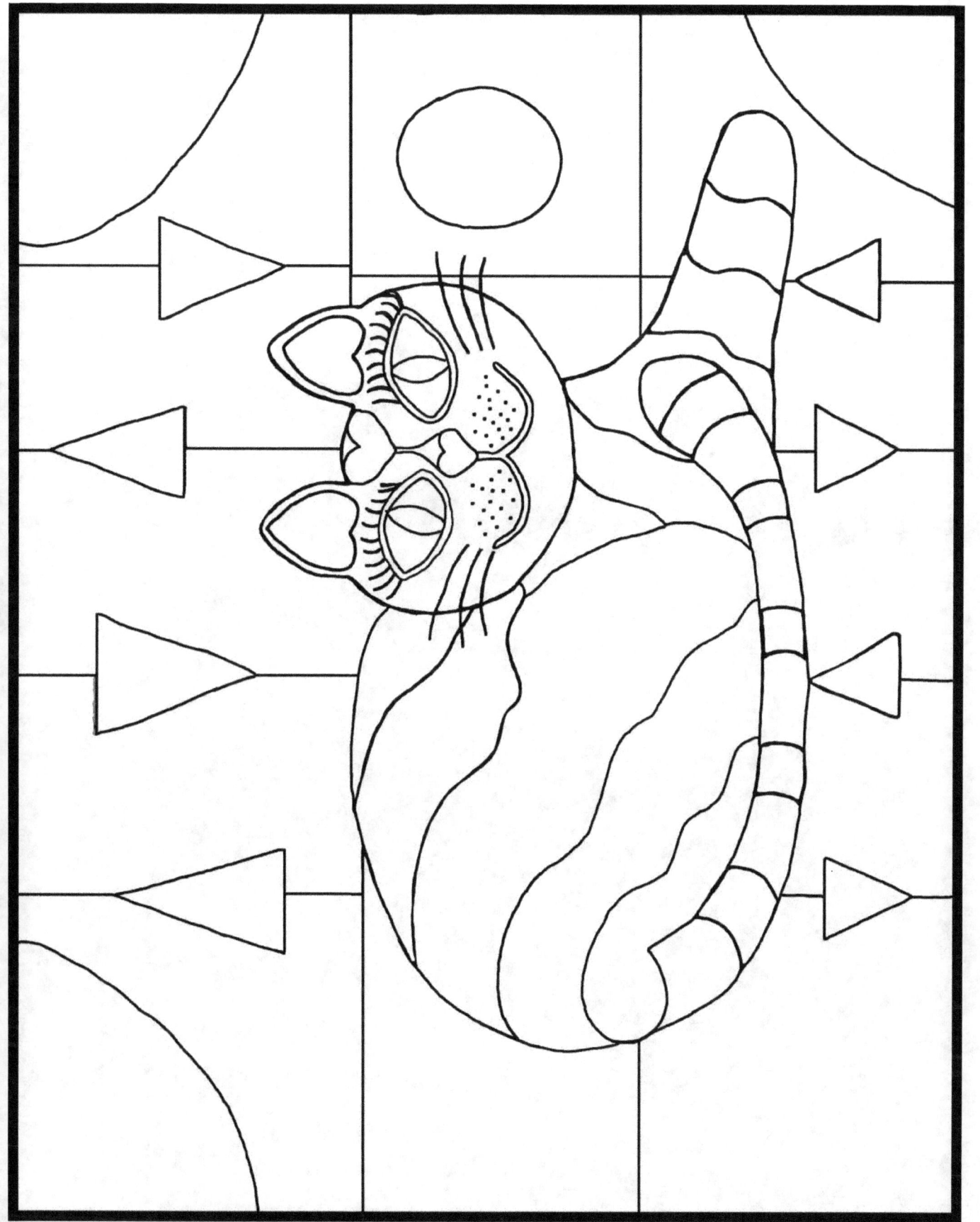

The Cats with Loving Hearts

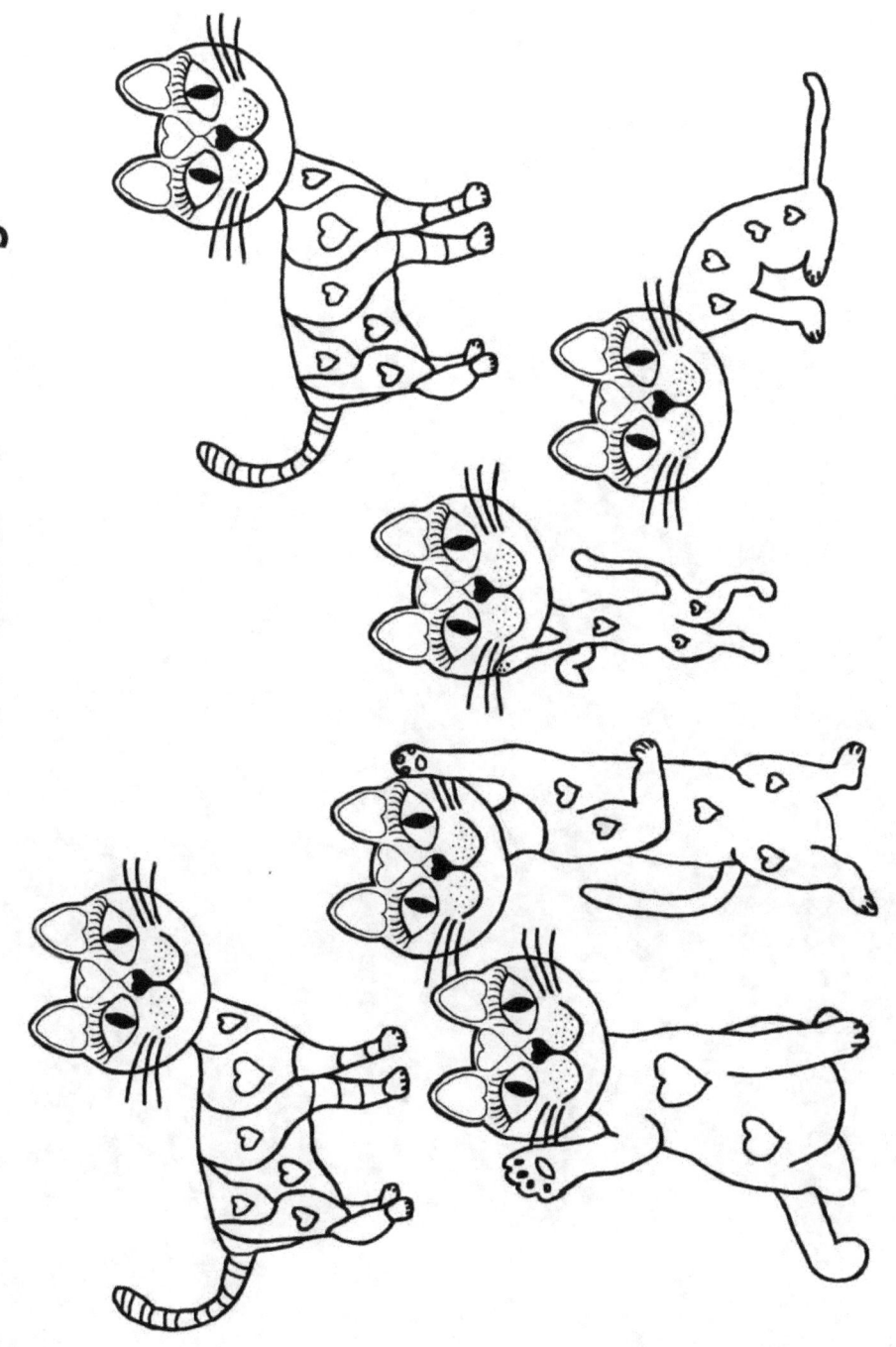

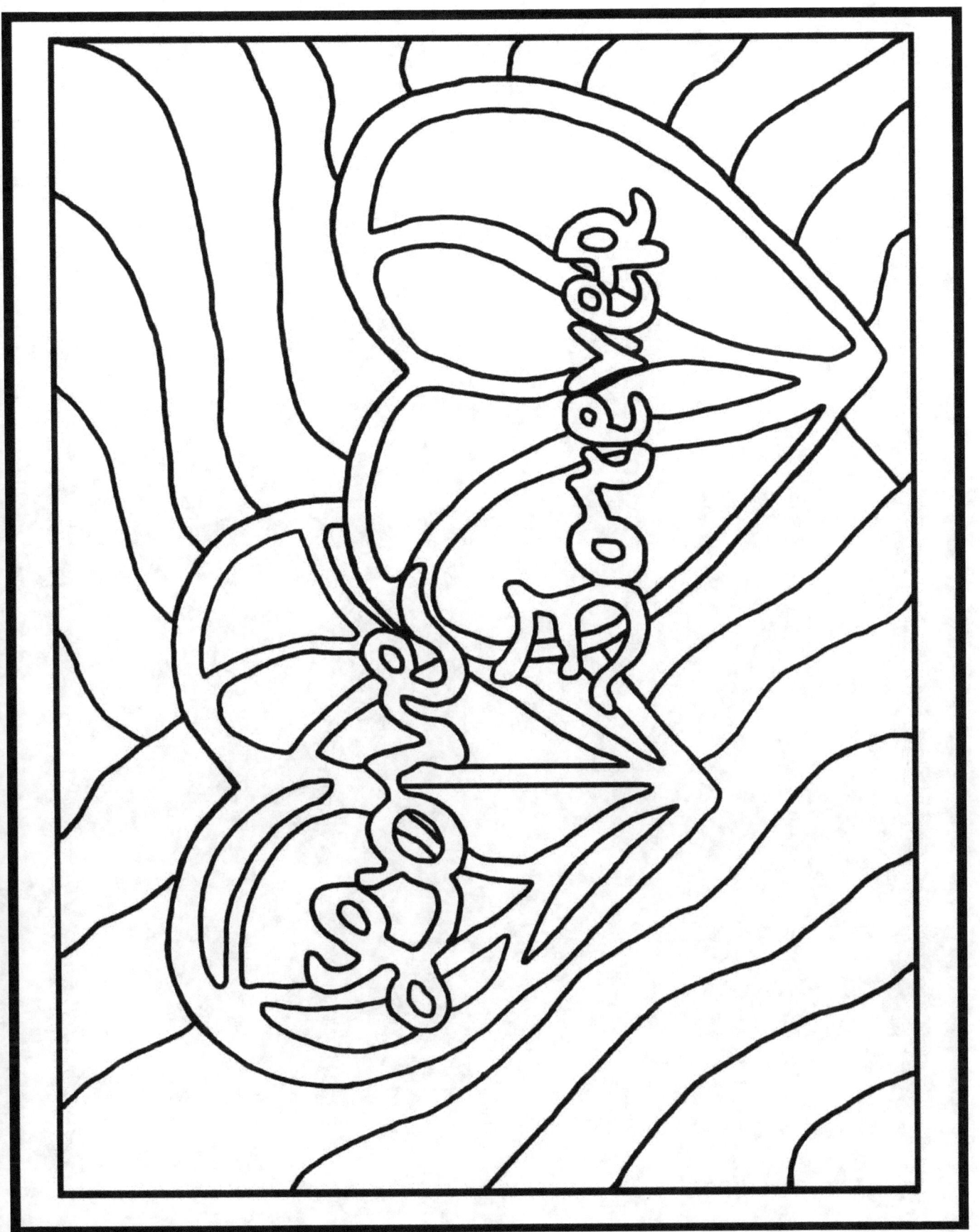

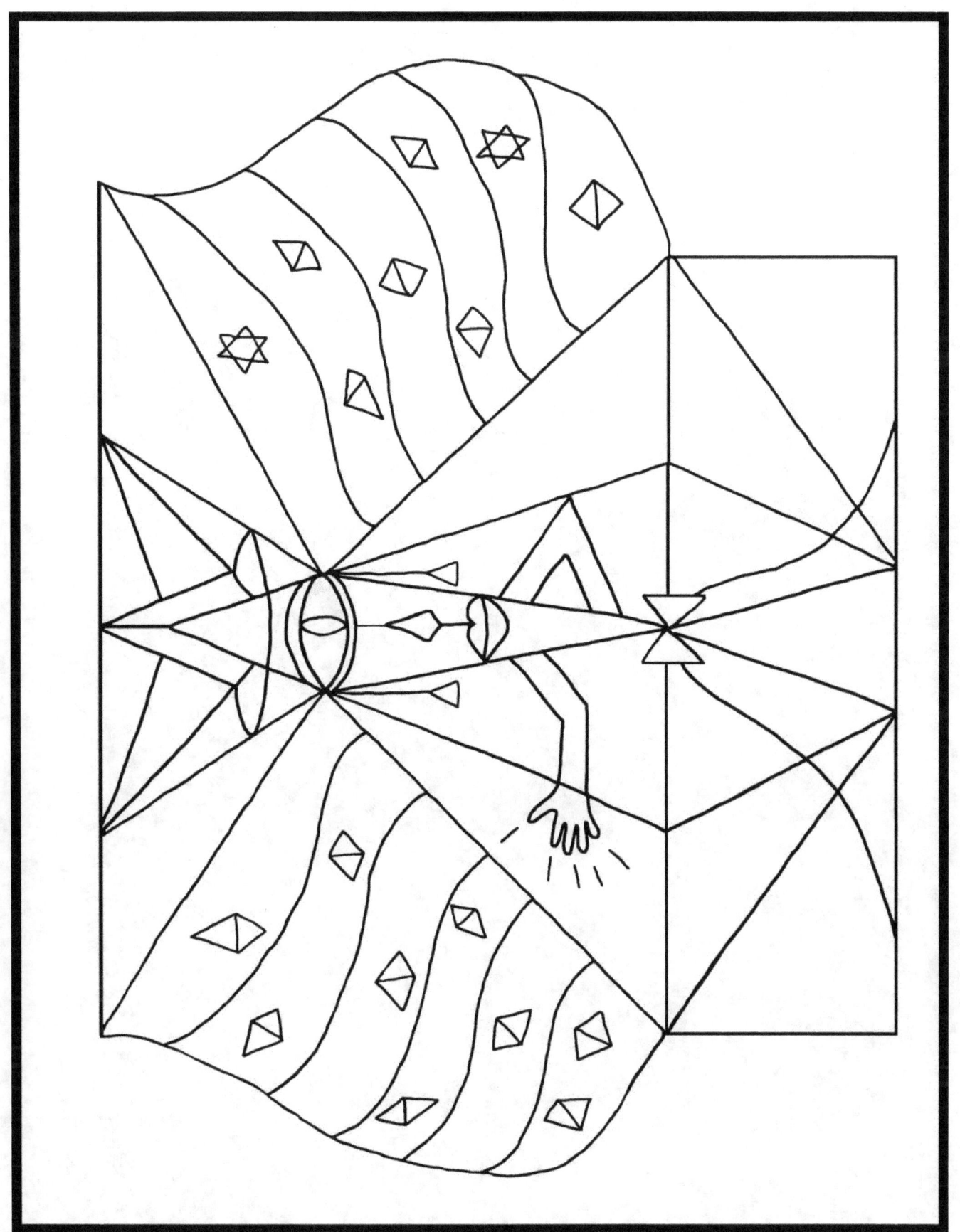

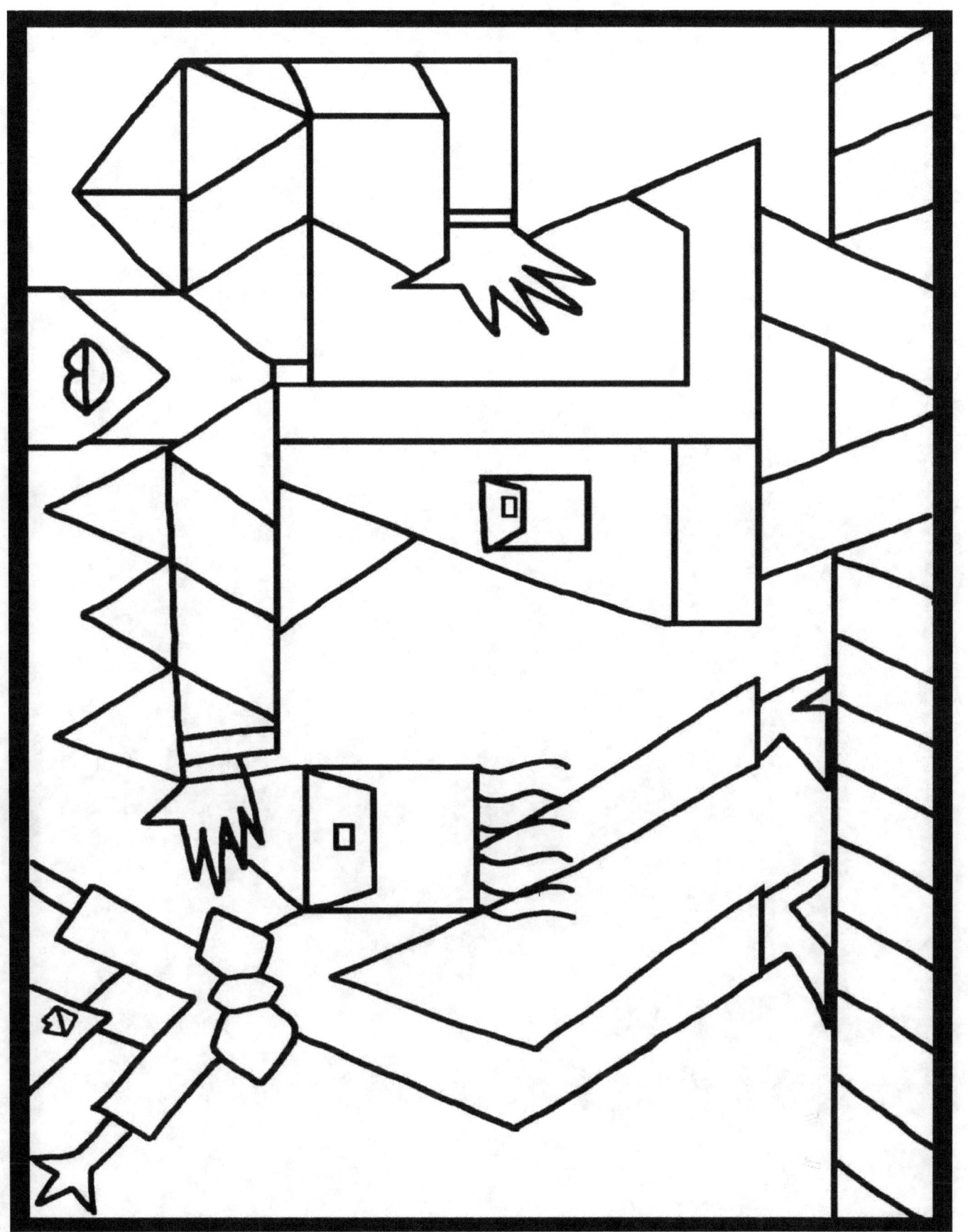

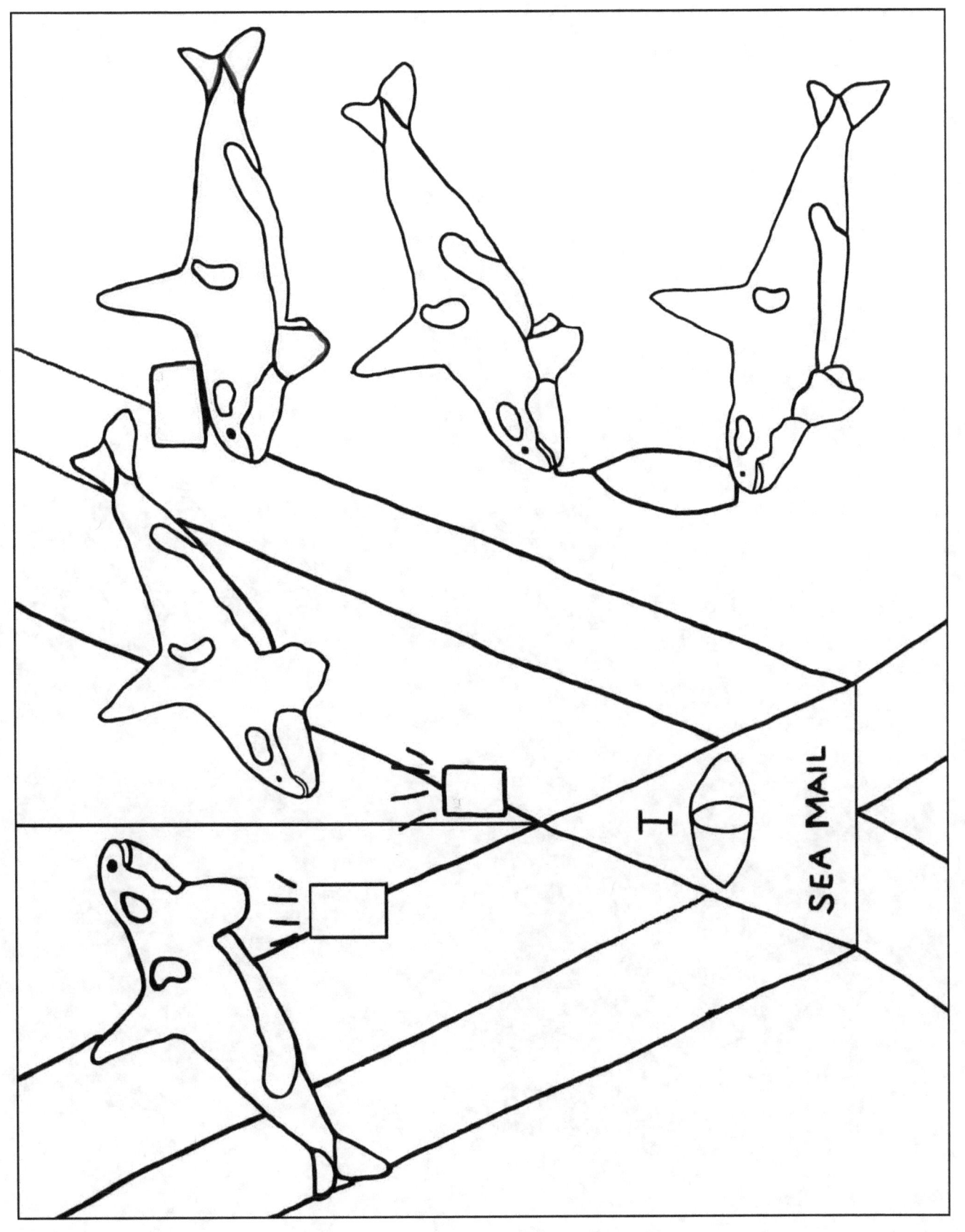

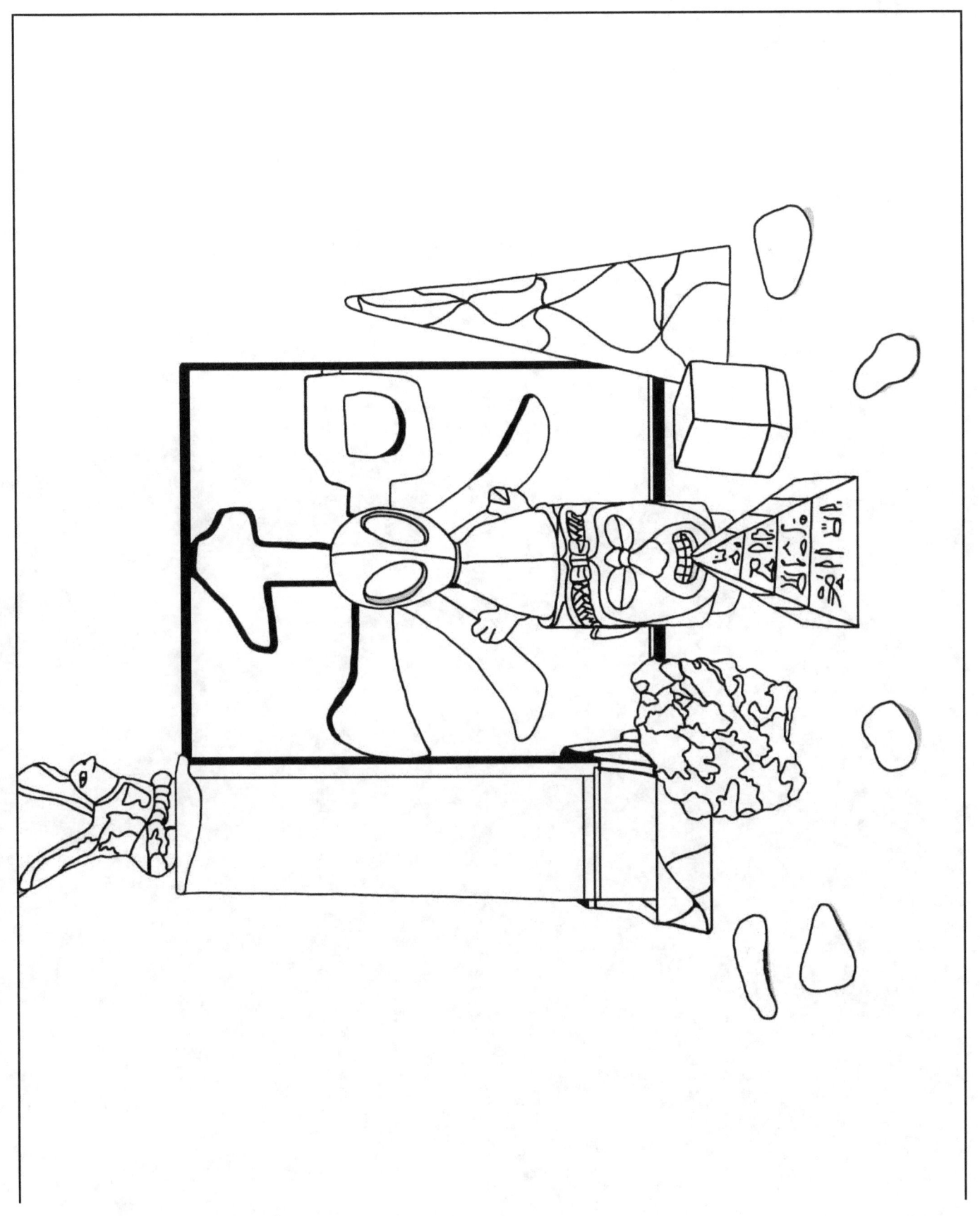

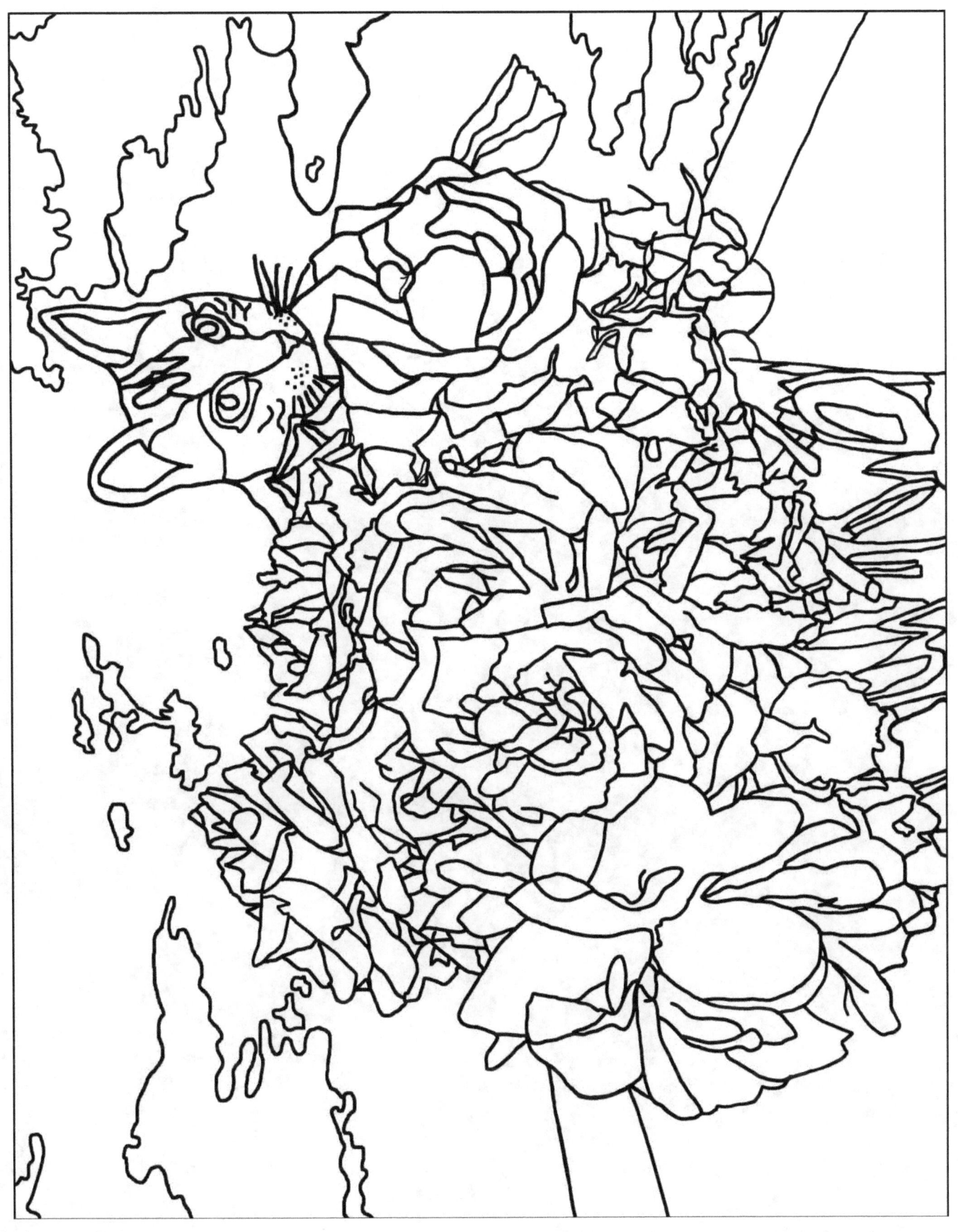

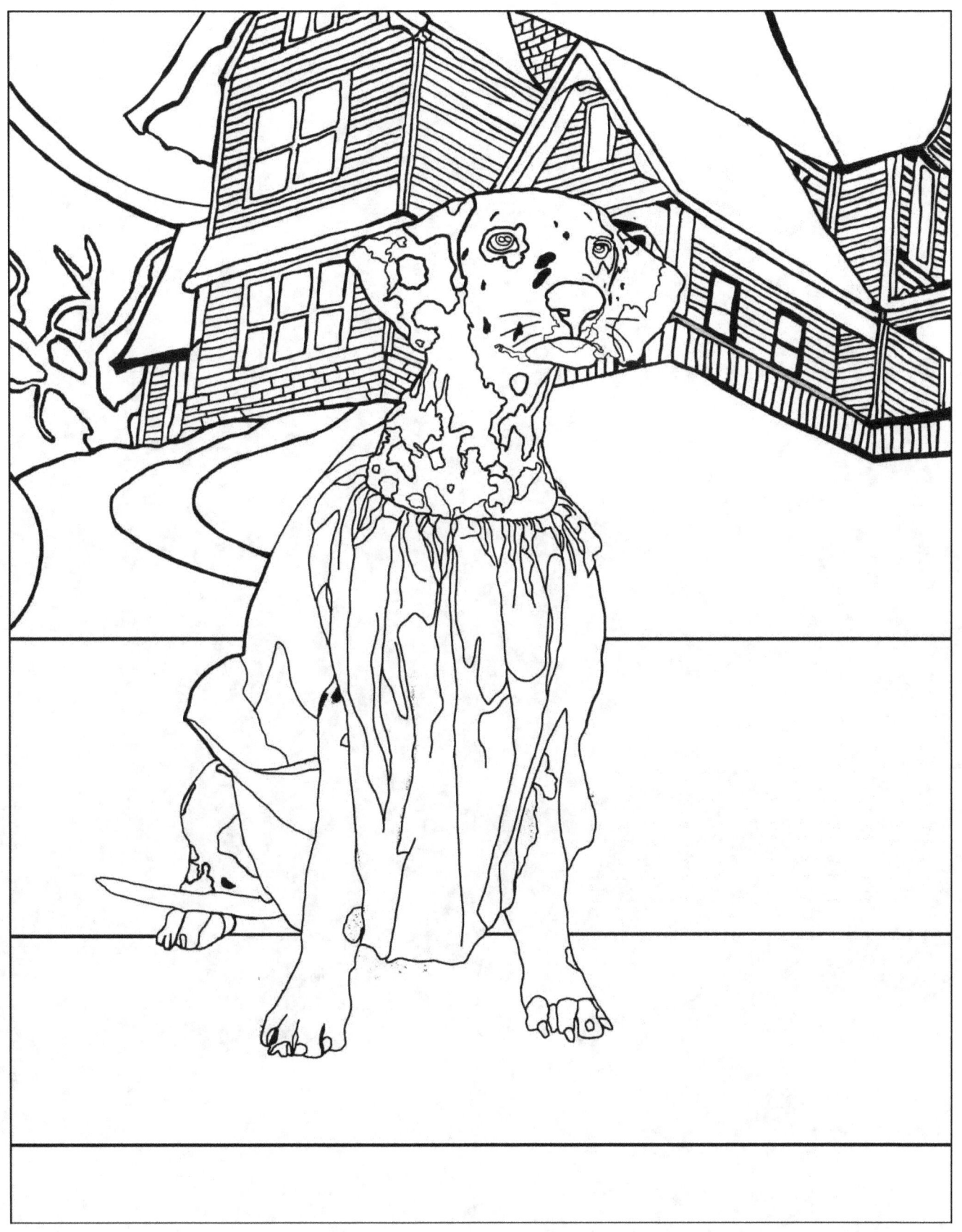

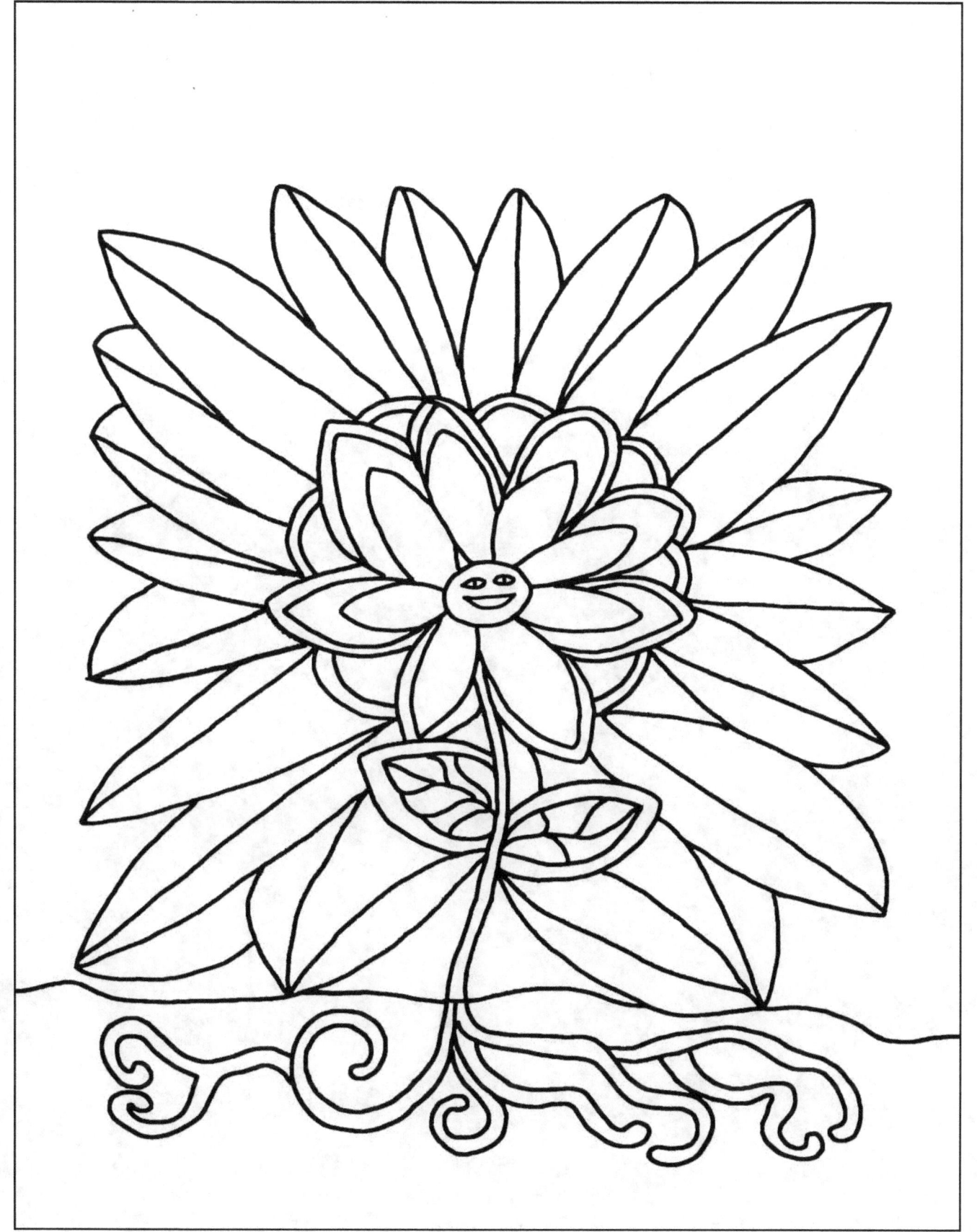

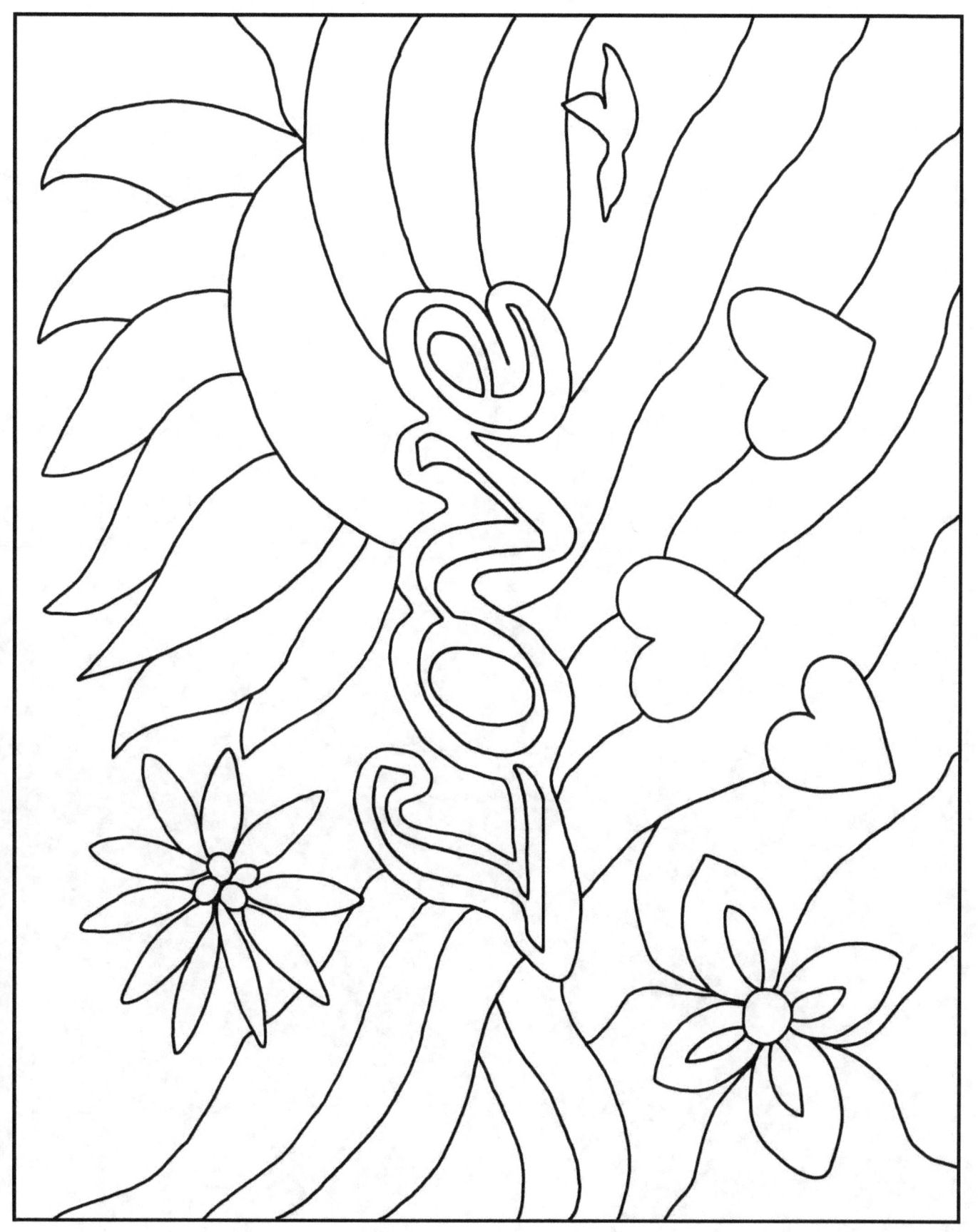

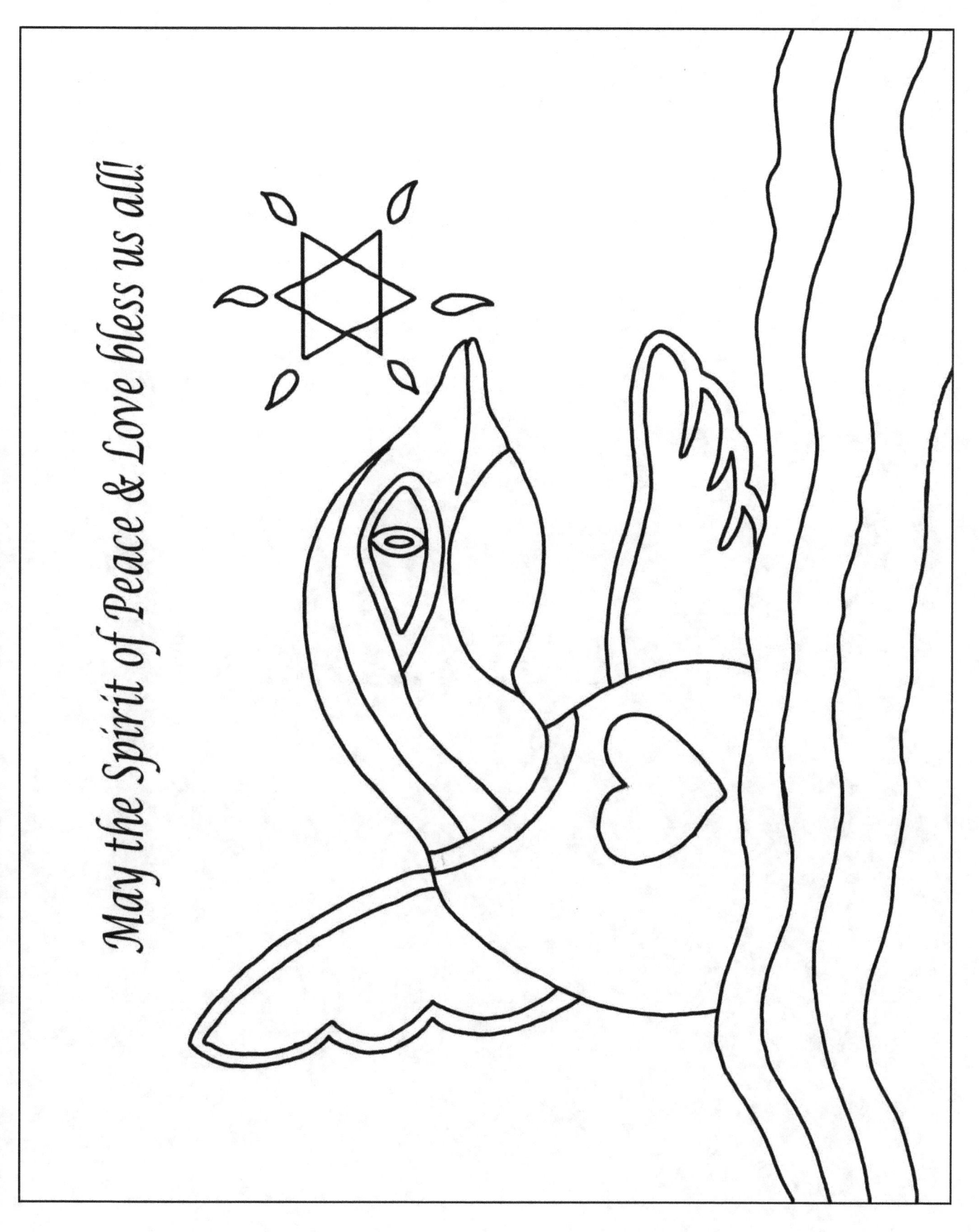

May the Spirit of Peace & Love bless us all!

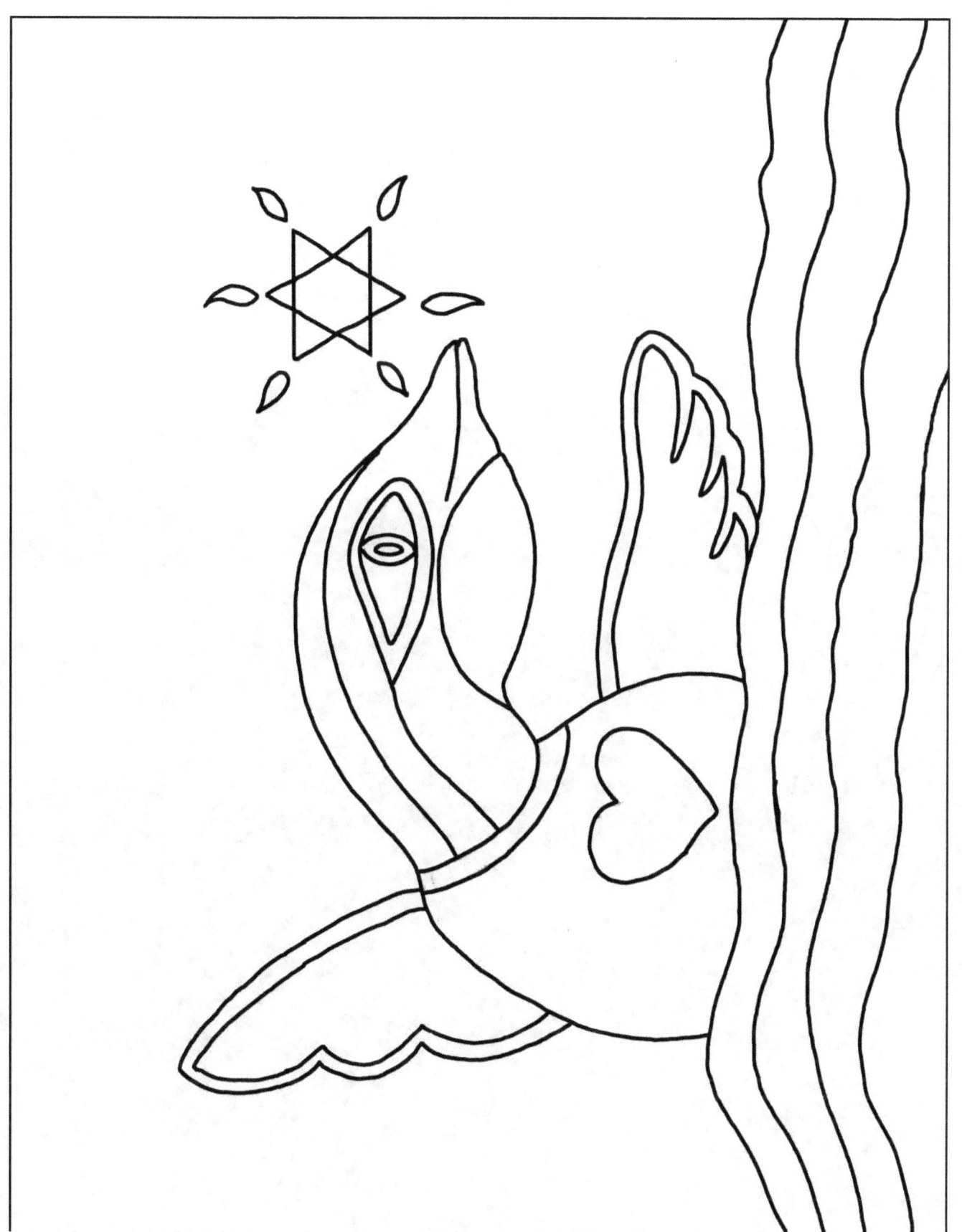

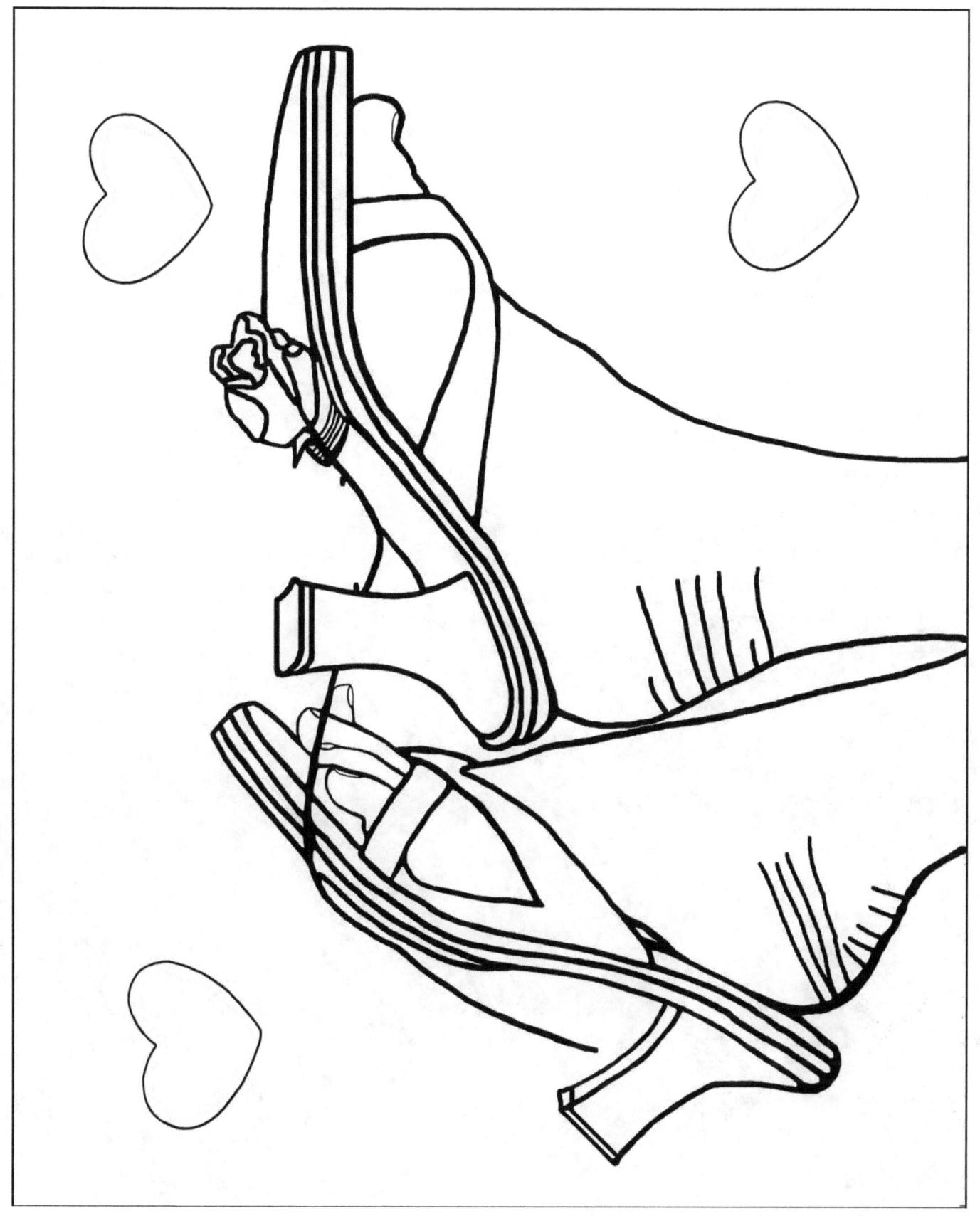

Other books by Laura L. Smith

Clicking for Cash from Home: How to start and run a home based photography business
Pink Kitty's Friendly Tales
The Cat Chat Forum

All books are available on Amazon

Products by the author:
Pink Kitty Lapel pin $3.00 + $3.00 shipping.
Pendulum and answer sheet $8.00 + $3.00 shipping.
Contact author at laural.s2012@gmail.com to order

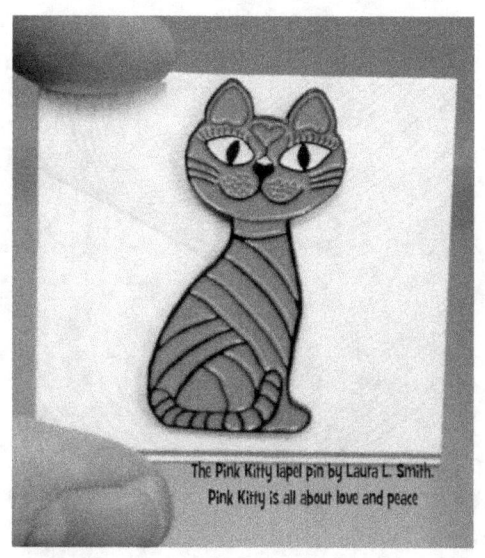

The Pink Kitty lapel pin by Laura L. Smith.
Pink Kitty is all about love and peace

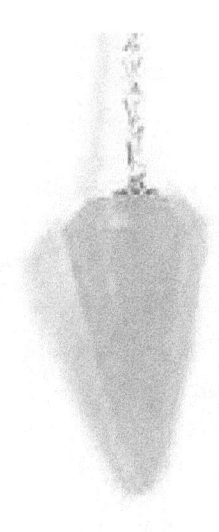

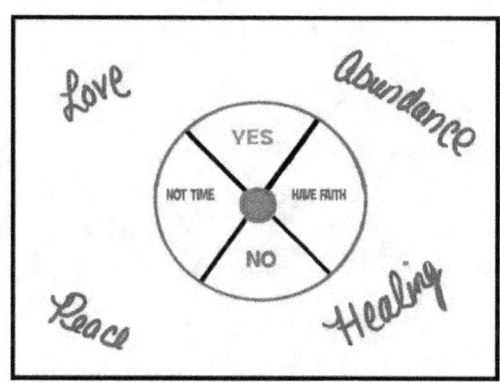